UNDERSTANDING ECONOMICS

A CASE STUDY APPROACH

TEACHER'S RESOURCE MANUAL

GLOBE FEARON EDUCATIONAL PUBLISHER
A Division of Simon & Schuster
Upper Saddle River, New Jersey

Director of Editorial and Marketing: Nancy Surridge
Project Editor: Carol Schneider
Editorial Developer: Curriculum Concepts, Inc.
Production Director: Kurt Scherwatzky
Production Editor: Rosann Bar
Electronic Page Production and Design: Jonathan E. Nathan

Copyright © 1997 by Globe Fearon Educational Publisher, a division of Simon & Schuster, One Lake Street, Upper Saddle River, New Jersey 07458. All rights reserved. No part of this book may be reproduced or transmitted in any form or by any means, electrical or mechanical, including photocopying, recording, or by any information storage and retrieval system, without permission in writing from the publisher.

Permission is given for individual classroom teachers to reproduce pages 87–96 for classroom use. Reproduction of these materials for an entire school system is strictly forbidden.

Printed in the United States of America
3 4 5 6 7 8 9 10   98 99 00 01 01

BF2

ISBN 0-8359-1811-4

GLOBE FEARON EDUCATIONAL PUBLISHER
A Division of Simon & Schuster
Upper Saddle River, New Jersey

CONTENTS

Introduction	4
Correlation Chart	8
Chapter 1	10
Chapter 1 Test	14
Chapter 2	16
Chapter 2 Test	20
Chapter 3	22
Chapter 3 Test	26
Chapter 4	28
Chapter 4 Test	32
Chapter 5	34
Chapter 5 Test	38
Chapter 6	40
Chapter 6 Test	44
Chapter 7	46
Chapter 7 Test	50
Chapter 8	52
Chapter 8 Test	56
Chapter 9	58
Chapter 9 Test	62
Chapter 10	64
Chapter 10 Test	68
Answer Key	70
Reproducible Worksheets	87

INTRODUCTION

Purpose and Rationale

Why economics? In 1994, the U.S. Congress included economics among the core subjects in which students will be expected to meet certain standards by the year 2000.

According to a recent Gallup poll, many high school seniors in the United States do not know what the federal deficit is, do not understand what profits are, cannot identify the most widely used measure of inflation, and do not know the present unemployment rate. In a time of political battle over the handling of the deficit, international trade agreements, and the management of inflation and unemployment, how can citizens vote intelligently if they do not understand basic economics?

In addition to producing responsible citizens, the study of economics can help students become productive members of the workforce, knowledgeable consumers, prudent savers and investors, effective participants in the global economy, and competent decision makers.

How This Program Works

Understanding Economics contains 10 chapters. Each chapter begins with a case study that is a real-life example of economic factors at work. The topics have been carefully chosen to include situations to which students can relate.

In Chapter 1, the case study presents a salad dressing and produce company from South Central Los Angeles, California, that is owned and operated by students. It introduces important concepts about resources and entrepreneurship.

Chapter 2's case study concerns three brothers who immigrated to the United States from China. It compares different economic systems.

In Chapter 3, the case study looks at advertising by using Nike and Domino's as examples. Concepts of supply and demand are introduced.

Chapter 4 discusses how minimum wage and labor laws affect a teenager working in a music store. It focuses on the functions of government in the economy.

In Chapter 5, students study the history of the Schwinn Bicycle Company, from its huge success to bankruptcy to comeback. In the course of the discussion, students learn about business organizations and the role of competition in the marketplace.

Chapter 6 deals with labor and wages. The case study profiles a Ben & Jerry's employee to illustrate the supply and demand of labor. The chapter also looks at the development of U.S. labor unions.

Chapter 7's case study outlines a young person's fall into credit card debt. The lesson teaches students the value of budgeting and the dangers of credit card misuse.

Chapter 8 looks at a young person right out of college who is getting a start in a big corporation. Students read about the choices to be made regarding company benefits and investment choices. The focus of the discussion is a comparison of investments: stocks, bonds, and mutual funds.

In the Chapter 9 case study, a teenager comparison shops for a portable cassette player. The lesson looks at consumer rights and responsibilities and encourages students to be informed consumers.

Chapter 10's case study of Coca-Cola shows what it takes to become a multinational corporation. The lesson discusses international trade, barriers to trade, and international trade agreements (NAFTA and GATT).

In each chapter, the case study is followed by a worktext that presents concepts and vocabulary. Students read and answer questions throughout the worktext and relate the concepts and vocabulary to the case study they have read. The worktext includes features called "Think About It!," "Check Your Understanding," and "Take Another Look" that reinforce the chapter's concepts and lessons. Each chapter also includes a one-page worksheet, "Using Economics Skills," that provides practice in reading graphs and charts. Each chapter ends with two pages of "Chapter Review" questions.

The *Teacher's Resource Manual* provides a motivating activity with which to begin each lesson, a list of terms covered, and suggested teaching strategies. The teacher is guided step-by-step through the chapter and given ideas for presenting or supplementing the information in the student edition. The *Teacher's Resource Manual* suggests ways of breaking down each chapter into smaller units over a two-week period, but teachers can easily cover more or less in one class period.

For each chapter, the *Teacher's Resource Manual* includes multicultural notes, guided discussion topics, and cooperative learning activities, all of which the teacher may use as he or she wishes.

Also provided are a two-page test and answer key for each chapter. At the end of the *Teacher's Resource Manual* are reproducible activity worksheets for the ten chapters.

Teaching ESL/LEP Students

Students for whom English is a second language or those who have limited English proficiency may benefit from these teaching strategies:

- Write new words and terms on the chalkboard as they are discussed. Repeat the word after you write it.

- In the earlier lessons, give examples of good answers to the first few questions in the student edition. Show students where to find the answers in the text.

- Make sure students understand how the case study relates to the lesson. Point out that the case study is a real-life example of a concept that they will learn about in the lesson.

- Have students make their own glossary of new terms as they learn them. They can take part of a notebook and set aside a page or two for each letter of the alphabet. This repetition will help them memorize the new vocabulary.

- When forming small groups or pairs of students, as is often suggested throughout the *Teacher's Resource Manual*, be sure to include native English speakers with those who have language difficulties.

- Look for ways to simplify and paraphrase explanations and give realistic examples.

- Encourage all students to respond to questions in whole sentences. Model this behavior yourself as much as possible.

- Ask students to share economics news or information from their native countries. They may know about economic conditions, the government's role in the economy, the types of goods and services produced, and whether there are U.S.-owned companies in their countries. For any topic covered, you can ask these students to share relevant information from their native countries.
- Read out loud or tape record the case studies so that students can listen while they read along. In this way, they can learn the correct pronunciation of words.
- When checking written answers in the worktext, help students to clarify and rewrite their answers if necessary.
- To help learners who respond best to visual information, research videos on topics in economics.
- Throughout the lessons, look for ways to connect the economic concepts to situations with which students can relate. Find out about their part-time jobs, favorite television shows, and the "in" products.
- If students are shy about large-group discussions, increase the use of small groups. Students from certain cultures may be especially shy in mixed-gender groups. Use both single- and mixed-gender discussion groups.
- Give students time to ask questions during each class period.
- Have students keep a journal of the class. In it, have them record what they have learned, how the material relates to their lives, and what they found most interesting about each lesson. This type of journal can benefit all students, but it is especially helpful to ESL/LEP students who may be reluctant to participate in class discussions.

Following are more specific ESL/LEP teaching suggestions for each chapter. If students don't know the answers to some of these questions, you might turn those into mini-research projects.

Chapter 1: Ask students from other countries to talk about goods and services available in their countries and how people sell what they make or grow. How do farm products get to the cities? Are there community gardens like Food From the 'Hood?

Chapter 2: After the class has learned the three basic economic systems, ask students from other countries to determine which description matches the system in their native countries. How is that economy different from the U.S. economy? How is it the same?

Chapter 3: Ask students to describe advertising in their native countries. Which are the most popular brands of sneakers and jeans? How is advertising in those countries the same as it is in the United States? How is it different?

Chapter 4: Ask students about wages in their native countries. Is there a minimum wage? Are there any work restrictions for teenagers? Is the government involved in worker safety programs? How does the government respond to unemployment?

Chapter 5: Ask students to talk about businesses in their native countries. Are there mostly small or large companies? Do all companies face competition? Explain. How do companies that have been in business for a long time adapt to change?

Chapter 6: Ask students to describe worker benefits in their native countries and how they compare to those of the United States. Are there labor unions?

How powerful are they? What skills do many people have? What skills are scarce? What types of taxes are collected by the government?

Chapter 7: Ask students how people in their native countries pay for items for which they don't have money. Are bank loans available? Are there other sources of credit besides banks? How easy is it to get a credit card? What can be paid for with credit cards?

Chapter 8: Ask students to tell you where people in their native countries put their savings. What is the name of the stock market there? How do people prepare for retirement? Does the government provide retirement benefits?

Chapter 9: Ask students where they shop in their native countries. What recourse do they have if they have been treated unfairly by a seller? Are there consumer agencies or government agencies to help them? How can they get product information? Where do they shop for better-than-average prices? What items are less expensive in their native countries than in the United States? What items are more expensive?

Chapter 10: Ask students if Coca-Cola is sold in their native countries. Has it been sold for as long as they remember, or is it a recent arrival? What other U.S. brands are well-known in their countries? How do these products affect people's image of the United States? How do ads for a particular product in their native countries differ from ads for that product in the United States?

Correlation to Standards in Economics
for UNDERSTANDING ECONOMICS: A CASE STUDY APPROACH

By the Year 2000, students will be expected to meet *world class standards* in economics. The National Council on Economic Education has created a list of content statements outlining the core requirements for literacy in economics. The chart below shows how the content covered in *Understanding Economics: A Case Study Approach* correlates to this list.

Chapter	Case Study	Statement
Chapter 1 Understanding Economics	Food From the 'Hood	Scarcity and Choice Opportunity Cost and Trade-Offs
Chapter 2 Economic Systems	A U.S. Success Story	Productivity Economic Systems Markets and Prices
Chapter 3 Supply and Demand	A Case for Advertising	Supply and Demand
Chapter 4 Government and the Economy	The Minimum Wage	The Role of Government Gross Domestic Product Fiscal Policy Inflation and Deflation Unemployment
Chapter 5 Business and the Economy	Schwinn's Comeback	Competition and Market Structure Market Failures Economic Institutions and Incentives

Chapter	Case Study	Statement
Chapter 6 Labor and Pay	A Worker's Strengths	Income Distribution
Chapter 7 Money and Banking	Sarah's Freedom from Credit Card Debt	Exchange, Money, and Interdependence Monetary Policy
Chapter 8 Investments and Your Future	Investing in Yourself First	Economic Institutions and Incentives
Chapter 9 Consumers and Economic Decision Making	Max Comparison Shops	Competition and Market Structure
Chapter 10 The Global Economy	Coca-Cola Expands Worldwide	Absolute and Comparative Advantage and Barriers to Trade Exchange Rates and the Balance of Payments International Aspects of Growth and Stability

Chapter 1: Understanding Economics

Motivation

Ask students if they are familiar with any community- or student-run businesses. What type of businesses are they? Are they large or small? Are they successful? If students don't know of any community- or student-run businesses, ask them about local entrepreneurs or small-business owners.

Have students form small groups. Ask each group to choose a local store or business with which they are familiar, such as pizza parlors, ice-cream shops, and music stores. Then have students discuss and answer the following questions: What resources do you think the owners needed to start this business? What types of problems (start-up, marketing, financing, etc.) do you think the owners might have had? Does this business/store seem to be doing well in your community? Why do you think this is so?

Food From the 'Hood (pp. 2-6)

This case study focuses on a small business, developed from scratch, to introduce students to basic economics concepts.

Assign the case study as independent reading. Tell students to focus on the sequence of events—the way one idea or development led to another—and what resources or people were needed along the way.

Terms Covered economics, goods, services, scarcity, microeconomics, macroeconomics, needs, wants, productive resources (or factors of production), natural resources (renewable and nonrenewable), human resources, labor, entrepreneurs, capital resources, production, trade-offs, costs, alternative costs.

Reading Comprehension After students have read the case study, discuss it with them to be sure that they have grasped the important points. Ask the following reading comprehension questions. Encourage students to look back at the case study for the answers.

1. What business is described here? (Food From the 'Hood is a student-owned natural foods business.)
2. How did it start? (Tammy Bird came up with the idea as a way of helping the community after the Los Angeles riots.)
3. Who started it? (The business was started by Tammy Bird and a group of students.)
4. What events/people caused the idea to change and grow? (Melinda McMullen gave the students the idea to sell the vegetables that they grew and to use the profits to start a college scholarship fund. Funding from the State of California Riot Recovery allowed McMullen to quit her job and work full-time for Food From the 'Hood. The Rebuild Los Angeles group awarded the company a $50,000 grant that helped it to launch its Straight Out 'the Garden salad dressing. Sweet Adelaide agreed to manufacture and bottle the students' salad dressing. Norris Bernstein helped the students set financial goals and market their salad dressing to supermarket industry leaders.)

Multicultural Note

Los Angeles is the second largest urban area in the United States. Its population is 14 percent African American, 0.5 percent Native American, 9.8 percent Asian American, and 39.9 percent Latin American.

Learning and Applying Economics

What Is Economics? (pp. 7-8) Divide students into small groups. Have them read and discuss pages 7-8. Ask each group to record the answers to questions 1-5. Then ask a spokesperson from one group to read that group's answer to question 1. Use a different group for questions 2 and 3.

On the chalkboard, write the terms *goods* and *services*. Have each group's spokesperson read its answers to questions 4 and 5 while you list them under the appropriate term. Place a

10

check mark next to items that are repeated. Encourage students to debate any disagreements on classification.

Think About It! (p. 8) This section can be approached as a class brainstorming exercise that will stimulate debate and help students clarify their definitions of *goods* and *services*. The class list should have more than three examples of each term.

Read and discuss the definition of *scarcity*. Tell students that they will revisit the concept of scarcity later in the chapter.

Microeconomics and Macroeconomics (pp. 8-10) Write the term *microeconomics* on the chalkboard. Ask a volunteer to read the definition on pages 8-9. Have students give you examples of economic decisions that they have made. List their examples on the chalkboard under the heading *microeconomics*. Possibilities might include whether to buy CDs or tapes, where to buy them, and how much money to spend. Examples of other microeconomic decisions are whether or not to get a job, or how much to charge for baby-sitting or cutting a neighbor's lawn.

Write the term *macroeconomics* on the chalkboard. Ask a volunteer to read the definition of *macroeconomics*. Have students give examples of economic decisions that are made by the local, state, and federal governments. List these suggestions on the chalkboard under the heading *macroeconomics*. This might be a good time to include a discussion of current events, especially if there is presently a controversy about budget cuts, taxes, interest rates, or spending on unemployment, education, or the protection of the environment. Ask students to answer question 9 independently and have them share their answers with the class.

The "Wants and Needs" section, including questions 10-16, can be done as a class discussion or in small groups. Assign the "Check Your Understanding" section for homework.

Productive Resources (pp. 11-14) Divide the class into three groups. One group will be responsible for natural resources, one for human resources, and one for capital resources. Assign one student in each group to act as its recorder. Have the groups read the material on pages 11-12, up to the "Take Another Look" section.

Have each group work on a presentation about its type of resource, including a definition and as many examples of this type of resource as the group can generate. The group that handles natural resources should include a discussion of renewable and nonrenewable resources. Each group should describe how its resource fits into the production of goods and services. Give each group time to present its work to the class.

Have students answer questions 20-21. Assign the "Take Another Look" section, questions 22-25, for homework.

The next day, ask students to describe an entrepreneur in their own words. Then have them reread the "Human Resources" section on pages 11-12. Ask them to tell how Melinda McMullen, Tammy Bird, and the students fit the description of *entrepreneur*. What ideas, responsibilities, and risks belonged to each of them? Students should refer back to the case study as needed. Then have them answer questions 26-28.

In pairs or small groups, have students read the "Production of a Product" section and work together to answer questions 29-31.

Next, ask students why they think Food From the 'Hood chose to make salad dressing instead of increasing its production and sale of vegetables. (The size of the plot was small; they did not have the space to grow more vegetables.) Encourage them to look back at the case study if they don't remember.

Have students reread the definition of *scarcity* on page 8. Write the definition on the chalkboard. Then ask students to think about the consequences of scarcity. How does the scarcity of gold affect its price? How does the scarcity of their own money affect them? Lead them to see that in their own lives, scarcity results in the necessity of making choices. Ask students to give you examples of choices that they must make in spending their own money, for example, the choice between seeing a movie or eating at a fast-food restaurant. Encourage them to share as many examples as they can.

The Four Basic Economic Questions (pp. 14-16) In small groups, have students read and discuss pages 14-15. Have them answer question 32 and the "Check Your Understanding" questions, 33-36.

Help students recall the definition of *trade-offs* (pages 15-16). Define the terms *cost* and *alternative costs*. Have students generate examples of these terms as they relate to their own lives. In small groups, have students answer questions 37-40.

Using Economics Skills (p. 17) During the last 15 minutes of the class period, show students the bar graph on page 17. Ask them to read the title and labels and to describe in their own words what information is given in the graph. Point out the horizontal scale and the vertical scale. Have students complete this page for homework.

Guided Discussion Topics

Use these questions to focus students' attention on the chapter's main points.

- How did the development of Food From the 'Hood relate to the 1992 riots in Los Angeles?
- What role did Tammy Bird play in the development of Food From the 'Hood? What skills did she develop in the students?
- What role did Melinda McMullen play in the development of Food From the 'Hood? How did her background help the students?
- What were some of the choices that the students had to make when they decided to start a business?
- Why was coming up with a clever name and logo important?
- What factor limited the amount of money Food From the 'Hood could make from selling vegetables? How did the students deal with this problem?
- Why was Norris Bernstein's expertise so valuable to the students?
- Why was it important for the students to reach financial and distribution goals?
- Is Food From the 'Hood a success? How do you know? Give some examples.
- Why do you think it is important to study economics?
- How is microeconomics different from macroeconomics? Give examples.
- Do all people have the same needs? Do all people have the same wants? Explain.
- How do needs and wants affect how a person makes and spends money?
- Describe how natural, human, and capital resources might be involved in the production of a television show. What do you think the role of an entrepreneur might be in the production of a television show?

- What are the four basic economic questions? Give an example of a business and tell how the four questions might be answered by that business.
- How does scarcity affect a person's economic decisions? How do you think scarcity affects the decisions made by a business or government?
- Eddie can use his parents' car only if he can pay one-quarter of the car insurance premium. He is in high school and decides to get a part-time job. Discuss the meaning of *trade-offs* and *alternative costs* in terms of Eddie's situation.

Chapter 1 Review (pp. 18-19)

Have students complete the Chapter Review. Encourage students to ask about any points that they do not understand. They may work in pairs or in small groups.

Chapter Review Project (p. 19) Have students begin the Chapter Review Project. Their goal for the first day is to mutually decide on the goods or services that they would like to provide and to discuss the qualities that they would like people to associate with their company.

The following day, allow students time to construct a statement of purpose for their project. Have each group present its statement of purpose to the class

Cooperative Learning Activities

1. Have students choose a mall, shopping center, or large department store with which they are all familiar. Have them make a list of goods and services that can be purchased at that location. Then have them prepare a poster or advertising brochure based on their lists.

2. Have students plan a baby-sitting or dog-sitting service. Have them describe how their service uses different productive resources. Ask them to discuss how their service would meet the needs and wants of their potential customers and of themselves. Have them include a statement about how scarcity might play a role in their business.

Chapter 1 Test Answers

(1 point for 1-10; 2 points for 11-12; 4 points for 13)

1. c **2.** b **3.** d **4.** b **5.** c **6.** good **7.** human resource **8.** scarcity **9.** alternative cost **10.** need **11.** the owner is a human resource; the shop, ovens, boxes, and most of the pizza makings are capital resources; the servers and cooks are labor and human resources; some of the food, such as the vegetables, could be classified as renewable natural resources. **12.** Answers may vary. You give up free time or after-school activities to have a job that gives you money. **13.** Answers will vary.

CHAPTER 1 TEST

Circle the letter of the best answer.

1. A person who starts a new company or introduces a new product is
   a. a human resource.
   b. a capital resource.
   c. an entrepreneur.
   d. an economist.

2. The study of economic decision making by individuals and in businesses is/are
   a. factors of production.
   b. microeconomics.
   c. macroeconomics.
   d. trade-offs.

3. Which of the following is *not* an example of a good?
   a. a sweater
   b. a computer
   c. scissors
   d. cutting hair

4. Which of the following is a capital resource?
   a. oil from a well
   b. a truck for deliveries
   c. farm workers
   d. cotton plants

5. Which of the following is *not* one of the factors of production?
   a. entrepreneurship
   b. natural resources
   c. climate
   d. human resources

Complete each sentence with the best term from the list below.

entrepreneur   **need**   **service**   **good**
human resource   **want**   **alternative cost**   **scarcity**

6. A product that people use, such as writing paper, a CD player, or a chicken, is a _____.

7. A person's ability to write computer programs is an example of a _____.

8. When people want more goods and services than they can have, there is a _____.

9. Having to buy a book for school instead of a ticket to a rock concert is an example of an _____.

10. Something that you must have to sustain your everyday life is an example of a _____.

Answer the following.

11. Use the following example to list and identify productive resources.

A pizza parlor opens. The owner paid three months' rent in advance and bought two special pizza ovens. He also bought sauce, cheese, flour, boxes, different meats and vegetables for toppings, and soft drinks. He hired a cook and someone to wait on customers.

_____
_____
_____
_____
_____
_____

12. Explain how the term *trade-off* applies to the decision to take a part-time job after school.

_____
_____
_____
_____
_____
_____

13. Your own resources of time and money are limited. On a separate sheet of paper, write a paragraph that describes how you deal with these limitations in terms of your unique wants and needs.

_____
_____
_____
_____
_____
_____
_____
_____

Chapter 2: Economic Systems

Motivation

Have students talk about relatives, friends, or neighbors who have immigrated to the United States. What do students know about living and working in the countries from which these people emigrated? How is life there different from life in the United States? Have students work in small groups to answer the following questions about a country with which at least one of the group is familiar: How do people in that country buy food, find a place to live, get a job? Are there items you can buy in the United States that can't be bought in that country? Are there items that can be bought in that country that can't be bought in the United States? Why do people immigrate to the United States from that country?

A U.S. Success Story (pp. 20-23)

This case study provides an opportunity to discuss differences among economic systems.

Assign the case study as independent reading. Ask students to think about the contrasts between the economies of China and the United States as they read.

Terms Covered economic system, tradition-based economic system, command economic system, market economic system, capitalism, mixed economic system, market, buyers, sellers, producers, consumers, resource market, product market, economic freedom, price, voluntary exchange, profit, loss, profit motive, private property, competition

Reading Comprehension After students have read the case study, discuss its important points and summarize them on the chalkboard. Ask students to tell you about Geng Wong, his family, his home town, and the economic situation in China at the time the Wongs lived there. Then ask the following reading comprehension questions. Encourage students to look back at the case study if they can't answer a question.

1. What type of work did Geng's parents do in China? (Geng's mother moved cement, sand, and rocks in a one-wheel wagon. Mr. Wong worked as a chef for a local factory.)

2. How did the Wong family get from China to the United States? (The family first immigrated to Hong Kong and then came to the United States.)

3. What role did Hong Kong play in their lives? (Hong Kong's economy gave them the freedom to choose their jobs and make more money.)

4. What type of business did the Wongs start in the United States? (They started a newspaper store.)

5. What plans do the Wongs have for the future? (The Wongs are planning more and larger newspaper stores.)

Multicultural Note

From 1820-1993, there were 1,108,154 Chinese who immigrated to the United States. Many of those arriving from the 1840s through the 1860s went to California to help build the railroads and mine for gold.

In that same time period, 1820-1993, there were 7,085,324 German immigrants—the largest number of people to emigrate to the United States from any country. In all, there have been 37,484,020 emigrants from Europe, 7,171,986 million from Asia, and 15,064,901 from the Americas. There have been less than half a million emigrants from Africa and less than 200,000 from Australia and New Zealand.

Learning and Applying Economics

Economic Systems (pp. 24-27) Ask the class to tell you how the economy of China, as described in the case study, is different from the economy of the United States. Have students recall the four economic questions that they learned in Chapter 1. List them on the board as they are named. Ask students to tell you how these questions are answered in China and then how they are answered in the United States.

Then divide the class into three groups. Each group will read the portion of text concerning one economic system: tradition-based, command, or market. Each group will then prepare an oral presentation on its economic system. The presentation should include a definition of the economic system and some examples of how it works. (You may decide to give students more than one day to prepare so that they can make a visual aid as well.)

Each group should decide on a spokesperson. The spokesperson will give the group's presentation to the class. After the presentations, all students should be able to answer questions 1-15 in the text.

Mixed Economic Systems (pp. 28-29) Begin with the "Check Your Understanding" questions, 16-18. (You might want to use this section as a quiz.)

Write the term *mixed economic system* on the chalkboard. Ask students what they think it means. Talk about how China's command economy now includes some aspects of a market economy. Ask them to list ways that the U.S. system is mixed. Point out that the U.S. government influences interest rates and provides some relief to people facing economic hardship. Also, business and industry leaders make many of their own decisions, but they must also follow government regulations about aspects of their businesses that affect U.S. citizens, such as pollution and worker safety.

Have students work in small groups to answer question 19 and the "Think About It!" section.

Markets (pp. 29-30) Ask students to define *market* and give you examples of the ways in which the word is used. Then have students read the economist's definition of *market* in the text. Discuss how the economist's definition relates to other uses of the word. Have students finish reading page 29 and the top of page 30. Have them answer question 20.

Take Another Look (p. 30) Next, write two headings on the chalkboard or an overhead: *resource market* and *product market*. Ask students to read this section. Then have the class brainstorm a list of examples of each type of market. Remind students of the productive resources or factors of production that they learned about in Chapter 1—natural, human, and capital. Assign the "Take Another Look!" questions, 21-23, for homework.

The U.S. Economic System (pp. 31-33) Tell students that the U.S. economic system has many features of a market economy and draw their attention to the list of features on page 31. Then divide the class into four groups and assign each group one of the following terms: *economic freedom, voluntary exchange of goods and services, profit motive,* and *private property*.

Ask each group to read and discuss the section of the text that explains their term. Give each group five minutes at the end of class to present what they have learned about their term and give some examples. Have the class answer questions 24-30 for homework.

Economic Functions of U.S. Government (pp. 33-34) Ask students to give examples of unfair competition. Encourage them to give examples based on their own experiences in sports events or contests. Then ask them to think about ways that a business may engage in competition that is unfair. How can the government help keep competition fair?

Have students work in small groups on the "Functions of U.S. Government in the Economy" section. For each government role mentioned, ask the groups to brainstorm specific ways that the local, state, and federal governments fulfill that role. The roles that are mentioned are protecting private property, protecting competition, easing economic problems, and controlling inflation and unemployment.

Have the groups answer questions 31-36 and the "Check Your Understanding" section.

Using Economics Skills (p. 35)

This page gives students practice in reading charts. They will learn that charts can be used to compare and display information. Have them use the chart to answer questions 1-6. For homework, ask students to find an example of a chart in a newspaper or magazine. Have them write three questions that could be answered by reading the chart. You may use these charts and questions later for an end-of-chapter quiz.

Guided Discussion Topics

Use these questions to focus students' attention on the chapter's main points.

- Why do you think the case study is called a "U.S. Success Story"?
- Was the Wong's hard work rewarded in China? Explain.
- What type of work did Geng Wong's parents do in China? What type of work did his mother do in Hong Kong? Do you think Mrs. Wong preferred the work in Hong Kong? Why?
- Why do you think the Wongs did not stay in Hong Kong?
- What did Geng have to learn in order to be successful in the United States?
- How were the Wongs able to buy stores?
- What makes economic systems different from one another?
- Which economic system do you think is best? Give reasons for your answer.
- Is the economic system in China today the same as when Geng Wong was a child? Explain.
- Why do you think that most economic systems are mixed?
- Why do you think that so many tradition-based economic systems are small?
- How do economists use the word *market*? Name two types of markets.
- What does economic freedom mean? Give an example.
- How is price related to the idea of voluntary exchange of goods?
- What is the profit motive? How does the profit motive affect decisions that a company makes?
- How is property viewed in the United States? in China?
- In what ways can competition be unfair?
- What can the government do to keep competition fair?
- How does the government protect private property?
- What can government do to ease economic problems?
- Why is the central banking system important to the well-being of the U.S. economy?

Chapter 2 Review
(pp. 36-37)

Have students complete the Chapter Review. Encourage students to ask about any points that they do not understand. They may work as a class or in small groups.

Chapter Review Project (p. 37) Discuss the Chapter Review Project. Students' goal for the first day is to decide whom they can interview for the project and to compile a list of questions to ask about the economic system of the person's native country.

Encourage students to ask questions about the types of work available in that country, how people find jobs, who owns the businesses and resources, who makes the economic decisions, and what happens if a person can't find a job. Students should conduct the interview before the next class meeting.

Have students share the results of their interviews. Have each group present what the person interviewed told them about his or her native country's economic system. Have the class discuss how that country's economic system is the same as or different from that of the United States.

Cooperative Learning Activities

1. Have a group of students choose a particular good or service. For example, they may choose goods, such as CD players or cars, or services, such as hair cutting or meal preparation. For that particular item, have them discuss how each aspect of producing that good or service would work in a command economy and how it would work in a market economy. Have them create a chart to show the contrasts. Give students time to share their charts with the class.

2. Have each group choose a particular function of the government with which they are

familiar. Ask them to brainstorm about how that function impacts on their lives. For example, students may want to discuss the use of public parks in their neighborhoods.

Chapter 2 Test Answers

(1 point for 1-10; 2 points for 11-12; 3 points for 13-14)

1. b **2.** c **3.** d **4.** d **5.** b **6.** a **7.** b **8.** d **9.** c **10.** a **11.** economic freedom, voluntary exchange, profit motive, private property. **12.** advantages: stability, people don't have to make choices; disadvantages: does not adapt quickly to change, does not grow rapidly. **13.** Answers may vary. Mixed systems work well to balance prices and provide a variety of goods. Most economic systems in the world are mixed because this type of system offers the most financial benefits to both buyers and sellers. **14.** The profit motive is the search for the greatest profit. Profit is the money made by a business after all costs have been paid. Businesses make decisions that will keep profits at their highest and costs at their lowest.

CHAPTER 2 TEST

Circle the letter of the best answer.

1. The actions of buying and selling result in a/an
   a. profit.
   b. market.
   c. economy.
   d. economic freedom.

2. Another name for a market economic system is
   a. voluntary exchange.
   b. democracy.
   c. capitalism.
   d. tradition.

3. In which type of economy are decisions based on custom?
   a. command economy
   b. an economy that is 500 years old
   c. mixed economy
   d. tradition-based economy

4. The U.S. economic system is a
   a. tradition-based economy.
   b. command economy.
   c. market economy.
   d. mixed economy.

5. In which type of economic system does a central agency decide what the country will produce and how it will be distributed?
   a. tradition-based
   b. command
   c. market
   d. mixed

6. In which type of market do producers pay individuals for productive resources that they need to make products?
   a. resource market
   b. product market
   c. free market
   d. labor market

7. People who create goods or services are called
   a. consumers.
   b. producers.
   c. capitalists.
   d. advertisers.

8. A store sells CDs for $15. Many people buy them at that price. This is an example of a
   a. product market.
   b. market economy.
   c. private property.
   d. voluntary exchange.

9. The money made by a business after all its costs have been paid is
   a. a market.
   b. economic freedom.
   c. a profit.
   d. a price.

10. The government slows down the economy by
    a. decreasing the amount of available money to loan.
    b. increasing the amount of available money to loan.
    c. buying more goods from companies for government use.
    d. providing fewer public services.

Answer the following.

11. Name four features of a market economy.

   _____
   _____
   _____
   _____
   _____
   _____
   _____

12. List some advantages and disadvantages of a tradition-based economy.

   _____
   _____
   _____
   _____
   _____
   _____
   _____

Answer the following questions on a separate sheet of paper.

13. Why do you think that most economic systems in the world are mixed?

14. What is the profit motive? How does the profit motive affect the decisions a business makes?

Chapter 3: Supply and Demand

Motivation

Ask students to think about their shopping decisions. How do they decide what fast food they want? Why do they buy certain brands of clothes, jeans, and sneakers?

Have students work in small groups. Assign each group a different product of interest to teenagers—jeans, fast food, sneakers, and sweatshirts. Have each group brainstorm reasons why they buy a particular brand of that item. Then ask students to select the one or two factors that influence their decisions most. Have them star those factors.

A spokesperson from each group will then tell the class what product his or her group considered and the factors it developed for choosing a particular brand. Have the class discuss the top 10 factors the groups starred.

A Case for Advertising (pp. 38–40)

This chapter provides an opportunity to discuss how variations in supply and demand affect the economy.

Assign the case study as independent reading. Ask students to think about advertising that appeals to them and how it influences what they buy.

Terms Covered demand, law of demand, elastic demand, inelastic demand, competition, supply, law of supply, supply curve, elastic supply, inelastic supply, production costs, fixed costs, variable costs, equilibrium price, shortage, surplus

Reading Comprehension After students have read the case study, review its main points. Ask the following reading comprehension questions. Encourage students to look back at the case study if they can't answer a question.

1. How was Domino's Pizza able to increase its sales? (Domino's increased sales with its 30-minute pledge and advertising.)

2. Why would someone choose Domino's over a local pizza place? (Domino's has a faster delivery time.)

3. How did Nike increase its sales? (Nike increased sales through advertising.)

4. Why did people choose Nike running shoes at first? (They were stronger, lighter, and more comfortable than others.)

5. How did Nike increase its appeal? (Nike used famous athletes in its advertising.)

6. What caused Domino's to lose business? (A 17-year-old Domino's employee was killed while delivering a pizza.)

7. How did Domino's management respond to the downturn in its business? (First, Domino's denied that the 30-minute pledge was connected to unsafe driving. Then it dropped the pledge.)

8. What did Domino's do to turn things around? (It focused its advertising on teenagers and revised its image to be "cooler.")

9. What contributed to the decrease in Nike's sales? (An aerobic exercise shoe that customers thought was bulky and clunky, and a move into the non-sports shoe market decreased Nike's sales.)

10. Describe how Nike responded to the downturn. (It used advertising to identify itself with what was "cool.")

11. Ask students to summarize the ways in which the Domino's story and the Nike story are similar. (Both companies increased sales after potentially devastating loses in sales.)

Multicultural Note

Hakeem Olajuwon, the NBA basketball player who led the Houston Rockets to the NBA championship two years in a row, has become an advertising spokesman for an athletic shoe produced by Spalding. Olajuwon was born in Nigeria and came to the United States to go to college. While his endorsement career has not taken off quite the way

Michael Jordan's has, he is beginning to appear in many ad campaigns, including M&M/Mars, Uncle Ben's rice, and Rochester Big and Tall.

Learning and Applying Economics

Demand (p. 41) Divide the class into small groups. Have them read the "What Is Demand?" section and answer questions 1-2. Ask students to think of three different situations in which two of the conditions for demand are met. Have them vary the missing third condition each time. Then have a spokesperson from each group report to the class.

Have the class discuss how each condition of demand might be considered by a company with a new product.

Law of Demand (pp. 41-44) In pairs, have students read and discuss "The Law of Demand" section and answer questions 3-5. Then have them answer the "Take Another Look" questions, 6-8.

Ask students to tell you what they think of when they hear the word *elastic*. Then have them read the definitions of elastic demand and inelastic demand in the text and answer questions 9-11.

Write the terms *elastic demand* and *inelastic demand* on the chalkboard. Have the class brainstorm examples of each. Assign the "Check Your Understanding" section for homework.

Level of Demand (pp. 44-45) Have students read the "Changes in the Level of Demand" section. As a class, discuss the meaning of level of demand and the factors that influence it. Ask students to think of real-life examples to illustrate each factor listed on page 44. For example, the level of demand for bell-bottom jeans was greater in the 1970s than it is now because people's tastes are different now. During the Great Depression, the level of demand for many goods was low because many people did not have much money to spend.

In small groups, have students discuss and answer questions 14-15.

Competition (pp. 45-46) Have students stay in their groups to read the section on "Competition" and to answer questions 16-19. Point out that the total number of pizzas sold each week, 500, is the same for the first three tables.

Ask the class to name 10 different products. Write them on the board. For each product listed, have students name its competitors. Ask students to describe how competition is good for consumers. Then ask them to debate whether competition is good for businesses. Assign questions 20-22 in the "Think About It!" section for homework. Remind students to come up with products different from the ones used in the class discussion.

Supply (pp. 47-48) Ask students to work in small groups to design a product to sell. Have them estimate the cost of producing that product and decide on a selling price. Give the groups about 15 minutes to complete this task. Then, have each group list its product and its selling price on the chalkboard. Ask each group to compute its profit if it sold 100 items at that price. Then raise everybody's prices by $2 per item. Have students compute the new profit on 100 items. Next, lower the prices on about half of the products listed. Ask the class: "If you had a company that produced all these products, what decisions would you make based on these price changes? Give reasons for your decisions."

Have students read and answer the questions in the "What Is Supply?" section. Assign the "Take Another Look" section for homework.

Elastic and Inelastic Supply (pp. 49-50) Remind students that elastic demand occurs when a relatively small change in price affects the amount that people are willing to buy. Similarly, elastic supply occurs when a relatively small change in price results in a large change in the amount producers are willing to supply. Have students read the "Elastic and Inelastic Supply" and "Costs" sections.

In the last group activity, students saw the effect of price changes on profits. Ask students to form the same groups. This time, have students make a list of production costs necessary to make the product they chose. Have them determine which of the costs on their list are fixed and which are variable. Give each group five minutes to present its list of costs to the class. There may be some class discussion about differences in classification. Then have students answer questions 28-31.

Level of Supply (pp. 50-51) Divide the class into three groups to focus on changes in production costs, changes in technology, and changes in the number of competitors in the market. Have each group read the "Changes in the Level of Supply" section. Then have each group prepare a presentation about the factor it was assigned. Give each group 10 minutes to talk to the class about how supply is affected by the factor it investigated. After the presentations, have students answer questions 32-34.

Supply and Demand (pp. 51-52) To be sure that students understand the graph on page 51, ask them to come up with some points along the demand and supply curves. For example, on the demand curve, ask students how many pizzas people were willing to purchase at $14 per pizza (1 million). On the supply curve, how many pizzas will be produced at $14 per pizza? (7 million). Have students read the "Supply and Demand" section. Then ask them to define equilibrium price in their own words.

Have students work in pairs to discuss shortages and surpluses and to answer questions 35-38.

Using Economics Skills (pp. 53)

Have students work independently on this page. Draw students' attention to the graph for Luckey's Hot Wings. Point out that the vertical axis gives the price per box. The horizontal axis shows the number of millions of boxes supplied and demanded. Ask students how many boxes are represented by ½ on the horizontal axis (500,000). Have students read page 53 and answer questions 1-5.

Guided Discussion Topics

Use these questions to focus students' attention on the chapter's main points.

- Why do you think a company might spend millions of dollars on advertising? How does the money spent on ads contribute to the company's profits?
- What did Domino's offer that its competitors did not? Why do you think this offer helped increase its business?
- While Domino's and Nike faced sales slumps for different reasons, their turn-around attempts were similar. Explain.
- Are the sales of some products more influenced by advertising than others? Give examples.
- Name three conditions that create demand for goods.
- How is price related to demand?
- Explain the difference between elastic and inelastic demand.
- Give an example of a product that has inelastic demand. Why is its demand inelastic?
- How does advertising affect the level of demand? Give examples.
- Does competition affect the price of a good? Does it affect the level of demand? Explain your answers.
- What factors affect the profit a company makes on a product? Name as many as you can. Give an example of one factor that a company has little control of and one factor that a company can control.
- How is the price of a product related to its supply? Why?
- Define in your own words the term *elastic supply*.
- What are production costs? Give some examples of fixed costs. Give some examples of variable costs.
- What are some factors that can cause the level of supply to change?
- What is the equilibrium price for a product?
- How does a shortage of a good occur?
- How does a surplus of a good occur?

Chapter 3 Review (pp. 54-55)

Students may work in pairs or small groups to complete the Chapter Review. Encourage students to ask about any points that they do not understand.

Chapter Review Project (p. 55) Groups should begin work on the Chapter Review Project by designing a simple questionnaire to survey people about what athletic shoes they buy and how much advertising influences their decision. Students may also wish to bring in copies of their favorite ads. Have students present the results of their surveys. Then have a class discussion about which ads are persuasive and why.

Cooperative Learning Activity

In small groups, have students devise a plan for increasing the profits of a T-shirt company. Tell each group that their company is presently selling 200 T-shirts a month at $12 each and the cost per shirt is $7 each. Have each group outline a plan that includes some of the concepts in this chapter—for example, raising the level of demand or decreasing costs. Each group should write up its plan and an explanation of why its plan would work. The groups should also predict how much profits will increase as a result of the plan.

Chapter 3 Test Answers

(1 point for 1-10; 2 points for 11-12; 3 points for 13-14)

1. b **2.** d **3.** a **4.** c **5.** b **6.** c **7.** a **8.** b **9.** b **10.** c **11.** (1) want and need for goods; (2) willingness to pay the price asked for goods; (3) ability to pay for goods **12.** Competition lowers the price, which is good for consumers. For producers, the resulting lower prices can mean lower profits. **13.** If there is a demand for a good and its price is lowered, buyers are more willing to purchase more of it. The lower the price, the more people are willing to buy until there is a shortage. **14.** If demand is elastic, a relatively small price change will affect the amount people are willing to buy. If demand is inelastic, a price change has relatively little effect on the amount that people are willing to buy. For example, the demand for milk is inelastic. Demand for milk doesn't change even when the price changes.

CHAPTER 3 TEST

Circle the letter of the best answer.

1. Costs that change as production increases or decreases are
   a. fixed.
   b. variable.
   c. inelastic.
   d. elastic.

2. An oversupply of goods at a given price is a
   a. profit.
   b. demand.
   c. shortage.
   d. surplus.

3. Willingness to pay the asked-for price is a condition of
   a. demand.
   b. production.
   c. profit.
   d. shortage.

4. According to the law of demand, as prices increase people are willing to buy
   a. the same amount.
   b. more.
   c. less.
   d. nothing.

5. If a relatively small decrease in price results in a large increase in sales, then demand is
   a. greater than supply.
   b. elastic.
   c. inelastic.
   d. variable.

6. An undersupply of goods at a given price is
   a. a profit.
   b. an inventory.
   c. a shortage.
   d. a surplus.

7. Producers of the same product are
   a. competitors.
   b. partners.
   c. sellers.
   d. marketers.

8. Costs such as machinery and rent are called
   a. expensive.
   b. fixed.
   c. variable.
   d. inelastic.

9. According to the law of supply, a decrease in price will cause
   a. an increase in production.
   b. a decrease in production.
   c. a decrease in profit.
   d. an increase in profit.

10. The price at which the demand curve and supply curve meet is called the
    a. fixed cost.
    b. variable cost.
    c. equilibrium price.
    d. elastic demand.

Answer the following.

11. What three conditions are necessary for demand of a product?

12. How does competition affect consumers and producers?

13. Explain how a shortage of a good can be caused by its price.

14. Explain the difference between elastic and inelastic demand.

Chapter 4: Government and the Economy

Motivation

Ask students to share their experiences looking for part-time work. How did they job hunt? What happens during a job interview? About how much money per hour can a student earn at a part-time job? You might take a survey of the number of students in the class who work, how many hours they work, the types of jobs they have, and the amount they earn per hour.

Ask students if they have ever applied for working papers. Who must have working papers? Where do they obtain the papers? What kind of information must they supply?

Then ask students to list any work restrictions that they know of for people under 18 years of age. Where do they think the regulations come from? Do they think these regulations are necessary? Encourage students to debate the pros and cons of these rules.

The Minimum Wage (pp. 56–58)

This chapter provides an opportunity to discuss the ways government affects the economy.

Assign the case study for students to read independently. Ask them to think about the role of government in their own lives.

Terms Covered public facilities and services, general welfare, taxes, fraud, unemployment, inflation, income tax, progressive tax, regressive tax, corporate tax, excise tax, indirect tax, direct tax, tariffs, Gross Domestic Product (GDP), business cycle, deflation, Consumer Price Index

Reading Comprehension After students have read the case study, ask the following reading comprehension questions. Encourage them to look back at the case study if they can't answer a question.

1. Why did Vicky wait until her 18th birthday to start working? (She didn't want to get a work permit.)

2. Why are there strict laws about teenagers working? (Before labor laws, many children worked long hours for little pay under poor and dangerous conditions.)

3. When was the first federal child labor law passed? (1916)

4. What happened to the law in 1918? (It was declared unconstitutional.)

5. When was the Fair Labor Standards Act passed? (1938) **6.** What role do the states play in regulating child labor? (All 50 states have child labor laws. When there is a conflict between federal and state law, the law that has a higher standard on behalf of the child applies.)

7. Is the minimum wage the same in every state? Explain. (No. All states must adhere to the federal minimum wage, but some have chosen to raise it.)

8. What made Vicky finally realize why it was important for the government to pass laws that regulate the employment of young people? (She spoke with Mr. Martinez about the conditions under which children worked before 1916.)

> ### Multicultural Note
> Many Mexicans come to the United States to become farm workers because the pay is better in this country than in Mexico. The only U.S. industry that can legally employ children under the age of 16 is agriculture. The legal age for children to work picking strawberries and potatoes is 10. The legal age for all other crops is 12.

Learning and Applying Economics

Government's Role in the Economy (pp. 59–60) Write on the chalkboard or an overhead the words *federal*, *state*, and *local*. Under *local*, list the different local entities that apply to your school—for example, county government and town, city, or village government. List as many as apply.

Now ask students to think of people they know who work for any of these levels of government. List job titles rather than names under each category. Then ask students to brainstorm a list of government job titles. Place each title under the correct level of government. If necessary, prompt with titles, such as FBI agent, garbage collector, or bank examiner.

Have students read pages 59-60 and answer questions 1-4.

Economic Functions of Government (pp. 60-62)

You might begin by reading the preamble to the U.S. Constitution:

We the people of the United States, in order to form a more perfect union, establish justice, ensure domestic tranquillity, provide for the common defense, promote the general welfare, and secure the blessings of liberty to ourselves and our posterity, do ordain and establish this Constitution for the United States of America.

As a class, discuss what each phrase means in terms of tasks that the government performs.

Then in small groups, have students read and discuss the first two sections under "Economic Functions of Government." Each group should answer questions 5-10. Have a spokesperson from each group read its answers to the class.

Regulating Economic Activity (pp. 62-65)

Have students read the "Regulating Economic Activity" section. Then list on the chalkboard the four ways that government regulates economic activity: "ensuring competition," "supervising working conditions," "protecting consumers," and "protecting the environment." For each category, ask students for a specific example of how the government accomplishes that task. Have them draw on personal experiences or their study of U.S. history. For example, the anti-trust laws of the early 20th century were aimed at ensuring competition. The laws about working permits for teenagers relate to the supervision of working conditions. Students may know about food inspections, safety regulations at factories, or the Better Business Bureau. As students name ways that government protects the environment, try to identify the level of government involved.

If students have questions about unemployment and inflation, tell them that those topics will be covered in depth at the end of the chapter.

Have students work in pairs to answer questions 11-15. Assign the "Take Another Look" and "Check Your Understanding" sections for homework.

Taxes (pp. 64-67)

Divide the class into five groups. Each group must read, discuss, and present to the class a description of one of these taxes: income, Social Security, corporate, excise, or tariffs. Give each group 15 minutes to read and prepare a five-minute presentation. When all the groups have presented, ask students to explain the difference between progressive and regressive taxes.

Take Another Look (p. 67)

Draw student's attention to the chart. Write the entire number for the first entry—$628,000,000,000—on the chalkboard to remind students of the size of 1 billion. Based on the class presentations and discussion, have students complete questions 19-27.

GDP and the Business Cycle (pp. 68-70)

Remind students that one of the four functions of government is to ensure economic stability. Therefore, the government must keep track of the economy.

Have small groups read and discuss "The State of the Economy" section and answer questions 28-29.

Then have the groups read the "GDP and the Business Cycle," "Unemployment and Economic Stability," and "Inflation, Deflation, and Economic Stability" sections. Direct students' attention to the model of the business cycle on page 69. Some students may note that the shape resembles a roller coaster. Ask them to name factors that they think contribute to growth spurts and slowdowns in the economy. How do they think the government can make adjustments? Students can then answer questions 30-36 and complete the "Think About It!" section.

In small groups, have students list consequences of the following situation:

Suppose there is a small city in which most people work for one of three companies. One of the companies goes out of business.

When students have completed their list of consequences, ask them to discuss which they think could be addressed by the government.

Next, ask the same groups to consider what would happen in their families if salaries stayed the same, but the cost of all meat and meat products doubled. Again, have them list as many consequences as they can.

Using Economics Skills (p. 71)

This page gives students practice in reading pie graphs. Another name for a pie graph is a circle graph. It is made by finding what percentage of the whole each item is. This type of graph is useful for illustrating how the parts relate to the whole.

For the pie graph on page 71, point out that the actual amount of taxes collected is not given. The graph only shows what percentage of each type of tax makes up the whole.

Have students answer questions 1-3 independently.

Guided Discussion Topics

Use these questions to focus students' attention on the chapter's main points.

- Why does the government regulate teenage employment?
- Did the United States always have a minimum wage law? Explain.
- What are the three levels of government? Give an example of a task that is performed by each of these levels.
- What are three public goods and/or services provided by the government? Which of these do you think is most important? Give reasons for your answer.
- There is sometimes controversy over federal regulation of forests. Some people believe that the government should protect forests and the wildlife those forests support. Others think that the government should not interfere with businesses that want to harvest wood from the forests. Which group do you favor? Give reasons for your choice.
- Name some ways that the government promotes general welfare. Do you think the government should do more or less of this type of activity? Why?
- What are some ways in which the government regulates economic activity?
- How can the government ensure competition?
- Some people say that the government imposes too many regulations on business that cause profits to be lower. List some guidelines that an impartial person could use to determine if a specific government regulation is worthwhile.
- How does the government pay for its programs?
- Why is the personal income tax a progressive tax?
- Why is the Social Security tax a regressive tax?
- What is the difference between direct and indirect taxes?
- How does the government keep track of the economy? Describe the Gross Domestic Product.
- What are two large problems related to the business cycle?
- How can a change in demand cause inflation?
- What benefits to the economy result when unemployment is lowered?

Chapter 4 Review (pp. 72-73)

Have students work in small groups to complete the Chapter Review. Encourage students to ask about any points that they do not understand.

Chapter Review Project (p. 73) Have students begin work on the Chapter Review Project. As a class, brainstorm and research a list of government services. Then divide the class into groups. Have each group select a local service to research. Have group members decide how they are going to find out if the service is useful and what people who use it think of it.

Then have each group summarize its research on its government service and compare and contrast it with the other groups' findings.

Cooperative Learning Activity

Divide the class into small groups. Each group should choose one of the three levels of government for its focus. Make sure that there is at least one group for each of the levels. Then have groups brainstorm ways that government is involved in the running of their school. What government regulations must be followed in curriculum? in employment? in food service? in fire safety? Have the groups investigate how their particular level of government is involved in the day-to-day operations of the school. Have students do library research or interview appropriate school employees to answer their questions. Have a volunteer from each group report its findings. Students can then discuss how services/levels of government overlap.

Chapter 4 Test Answers

(1 point for 1-10; 2 points for 11-12; 3 points for 13-14)

1. c **2.** d **3.** b **4.** d **5.** c **6.** c **7.** a **8.** c **9.** d **10.** c **11.** (1) provide public well-being; (2) provide public facilities and services; (3) regulate economic activity; (4) ensure economic stability **12.** (1) establishes minimum wage; (2) establishes health and safety standards; (3) passes laws against discrimination **13.** Answers may vary. Government should increase the amount of money provided for education. Many urban schools are overcrowded and in poor condition. **14.** Answers may vary. Taxes should be assigned fairly so that people who cannot afford to pay too much do not end up paying too much. Nobody likes to pay taxes, but they are more willing to if they believe everyone is paying his or her fair share.

CHAPTER 4 TEST

Circle the letter of the best answer.

1. Which of the following is *not* an example of a public good or service?
   a. parks
   b. bridges
   c. commercial TV game shows
   d. U.S. Coast Guard

2. Another name for the well-being of all citizens is
   a. good citizenship.
   b. consumer protection.
   c. public service.
   d. general welfare.

3. Which of the following provides payments to workers who have been injured on the job?
   a. personal tax
   b. workers' compensation
   c. corporate tax
   d. Medicare

4. Which of the following is a task of the Food and Drug Administration?
   a. setting prices for prescription drugs
   b. setting prices for food
   c. keeping track of how much food people eat per year
   d. making sure that drugs that are sold are safe

5. Which government agency ensures that businesses do not pollute the water supply?
   a. the local water company
   b. the Department of Labor
   c. the Environmental Protection Agency
   d. the Internal Revenue Service

6. A sustained increase in the average level of prices in the whole economy is
   a. supply.
   b. demand.
   c. inflation.
   d. deflation.

7. The tax that all citizens pay as a percentage of their yearly income is
   a. a personal income tax.
   b. a corporate tax.
   c. an excise tax.
   d. a tariff.

8. The tax that a person pays when buying gasoline is called
   a. a personal income tax.
   b. a corporate income tax.
   c. an excise tax.
   d. a tariff.

9. A tax that takes a higher percentage of earnings from those with lower incomes is
   a. a personal income tax.
   b. a progressive tax.
   c. an excise tax.
   d. a regressive tax.

10. A measure that compares average prices in one year with those of an earlier year is
    a. the Gross Domestic Product.
    b. inflation.
    c. the Consumer Price Index.
    d. the Dow Jones Average.

Answer the following.

11. List the four economic functions of government.

    _____
    _____
    _____
    _____

12. List three ways that the government supervises working conditions.

    _____
    _____
    _____

13. Name a government service that you think should be provided or increased. Give reasons for your answer.

    _____
    _____
    _____

14. Why do you think it is important that taxes are assigned fairly?

    _____
    _____
    _____

Chapter 5: Business and the Economy

Motivation

Ask volunteers to share information about the styles, brands, and prices of their bicycles. Where did they buy their bikes? Where do they ride them?

Divide students into small groups to discuss a company that makes bicycles. What resources do they think the company needs to produce bikes? Where should it advertise to attract potential customers? What types of bicycles are most popular today? Have a spokesperson from each group present the results of its discussion.

Schwinn's Comeback (pp. 74-77)

In considering the upturns and downturns of the Schwinn company, students will be reviewing lessons from previous chapters concerning entrepreneurship, productive resources, supply, demand, and competition. This chapter introduces material about the forms of business organizations that exist in the United States.

Have students read the case study. Ask them to think about how Schwinn changed over its long history.

Terms Covered expenses, financial capital, investors, interest, sole proprietorship, partnership, general partnership, limited partnership, corporation, stockholder, charter, risk, board of directors, chief executive officer (CEO), bond, stock, share, dividend, perfect competition, monopoly, geographical monopolies, natural monopolies, technological monopolies, patent, monopolistic competition, oligopoly

Reading Comprehension After students have read the case study, discuss it with them to be sure that they have grasped its main points. Ask the following reading comprehension questions. Encourage students to look back at the case study if they can't answer a question.

1. What were the reasons for Schwinn's original success? (The bicycle was a cheaper alternative to the horse. Schwinn concentrated on the children's market. Its reputation for quality was unmatched.)

2. How did Schwinn respond to the competition from automobiles? (Schwinn focused its marketing strategy on children.)

3. How long did Schwinn have a dominant share of the bicycle market? (Schwinn dominated the bicycle market from the late 1800s through the mid-1970s.)

4. When did the decline in Schwinn's sales start? (It started in the late 1970s but went downhill in the early 1990s.)

5. Why did the decline happen? (Schwinn's market share declined because it refused to take the trend toward mountain bikes seriously.)

6. Who is Sam Zell and how did he enter the Schwinn picture? (Sam Zell is the multimillionaire who bought Schwinn.)

7. What were some of the changes the new management made to turn Schwinn around? (First, they moved the company to Boulder, Colorado, the center of one of the country's largest mountain-biking communities. Then they cut the work force from 300 to 180 and started redesigning the product—with an emphasis on mountain bikes.)

8. Do you think these changes will work? Why? (Yes. Schwinn still has great name recognition with baby boomers—the ones who are now buying bikes for their children—and because it is finally giving people what they want—a well-made mountain bike.)

Multicultural Note

In 1958, two entrepreneurs, Arthur Melin and Richard Knerr, took an idea from Australia and turned it into a giant toy fad. In Australia, gym students exercised using bamboo hoops. Melin and Knerr made round plastic tubes that could be rotated around the waist or neck, jumped through, or used as a jump rope. Thus, the Hula Hoop was born and 25 million were sold in its first four months on the market.

Competition and Market Structure (pp. 78–79) Have students work in small groups to read the "Competition and Market Structure" section. For each of the items listed under the "To get started, you will need:" passage, ask groups to come up with a specific list of considerations. For example, what factors should they consider when looking for a location? Where should they advertise? What employees will they need? Give each group five minutes to present its ideas about starting a bicycle business.

Then write "Start-Up Money" on the chalkboard. Ask students what they would have to buy or pay for before they could sell their first bicycle. As students brainstorm a list, write their ideas on the chalkboard. Then have students categorize each item as a one-time start-up cost or as an ongoing business expense.

Have students read the "Capital and Interest" section. Ask them why they think banks are willing to loan start-up money to businesses. Discuss loans and interest and their advantages and disadvantages to a business.

Then have students complete questions 1–5 in the text.

Business Structures (pp. 79–81) Have students work with a partner or in small groups. Ask them to read the "Types of Business Structures" section. Then have each group write the name and description of a business in each of the three categories—sole proprietorship, general partnership, corporation. Remind them to think about places where their family and friends work. If they can't think of a business for each of the structures, you might make the following suggestions: a newsstand is often a sole proprietorship, a law office is often a partnership, and many of the companies discussed already in the text, such as Nike and Domino's, are corporations.

Then have each group describe the business it listed under sole proprietorship. Ask the class to note differences and similarities among the businesses the groups listed in that category. Do the same for each of the other types of businesses.

Sketch a circle graph on the chalkboard or an overhead to illustrate the figures about U.S. businesses given at the top of page 80. Mark off a sector that is a little less than three-fourths of the circle (70 percent) and label it "Sole Proprietorships." Of the remaining sector, mark off one-third (10 percent) of it and label it "Partnerships." Label the other two-thirds (20 percent) of that sector "Corporations." In this way, students can see that the overwhelming percentage of businesses in the United States are sole proprietorships.

Ask students to read the "Running a Corporation" section. Ask volunteers to describe how each of the three types of businesses relates to risk. Students may work in small groups to answer questions 6–10. Assign the "Take Another Look" section for homework.

Corporate Organization (pp. 82–84) In small groups, have students read the "Organization of a Corporation" section. Ask them to pick a particular product or service and make an organizational chart for a corporation that would produce that product or service. Have the groups discuss and answer questions 14–16.

Have students read about stocks and bonds in the section "How Corporations Raise Capital." Ask them how they think investors decide whether to buy bonds or stocks. Are the risks the same for both? From which might an investor earn more money? Then ask them to answer questions 17–18.

Free Markets and Competition (pp. 84–85) Ask students to recall what they learned about competition and prices in Chapter 3. How does competition affect prices? Is competition good for consumers? Do you think a business prefers to have competition or not? Why?

Ask students to read the "Free Markets and Competition" section.

As a class, consider each of the factors required for perfect competition. For each factor, ask students to tell how they think the lack of that particular factor could interfere with competition. For example, if the product is a necessity, such as electrical power, buyers are not free to leave the market.

Have students answer questions 19–20. Assign the "Check Your Understanding" section as a group assignment or for homework.

Monopolies (pp. 85–88) Write the word *monopoly* on the chalkboard. Underline the prefix *mono*. Some students may recognize that it is the Greek word for "one." The root of the word, *poly*, comes from the Greek word *polein*, meaning "to sell." Ask students what they think the effect on the price of an item would be if only one company sold that item.

35

Divide the class into three groups. Ask each group to prepare a description of one of the legal monopolies: geographical, natural, or technological. Their descriptions must include a statement about why it makes sense for that type of monopoly to be legal. Have each group describe its type of monopoly to the class and answer any questions. Then have the class answer questions 25-28.

Next, have students read the "Imperfect Competition" section. Brainstorm with the class to think of examples of monopolistic competition and oligopoly. (Point out that the prefix *olig* is from the Greek word for "few.") Have students answer questions 29-31. Assign the "Think About It!" section for homework.

Using Economics Skills (p. 89)

This page gives students practice in reading line graphs. Line graphs are usually used to show how a quantity changes over time. Make sure that students understand the two scales. The horizontal axis shows years and the vertical axis shows Schwinn's share of the bicycle market. Have students answer questions 1-5 independently.

For homework, ask students to find an example of a line graph in a newspaper or magazine. Have them make up three questions that can be answered with the graph. Students can exchange their graphs and answer each other's questions for extra credit.

Guided Discussion Topics

Use these questions to focus students' attention on the chapter's main points.

- How did Schwinn respond to the changes in the bicycle market during the late 1970s?
- Why did Sam Zell change the company headquarters to Boulder, Colorado, from its original base in Chicago? How were new Schwinn employees different from the former ones?
- Name some business start-up costs. Name some business expenses.
- When the government wants to give the economy a boost, it lowers interest rates. How do you think this strategy works?
- What are some advantages and disadvantages of a sole proprietorship?
- What is the difference between a general partnership and a limited partnership?
- How is risk different for the three types of businesses?
- How are stockholders involved in the running of a corporation?
- What do you think the phrase *layers of management* means?
- How do corporations raise capital?
- What is perfect competition?
- Suppose there were only one company in the United States that knew how to make CDs. Do you think it could charge $25 for a CD? What do you think would happen if it charged $100 for a CD? Can a monopoly really charge any price it wants?
- What is a geographical monopoly? Can you think of any examples in our community?
- What is a natural monopoly?
- What is a technological monopoly?
- What is monopolistic competition?
- What is an oligopoly?
- Why is it difficult for an economy to provide perfect competition? If perfect competition did exist for a particular product, what might happen that could result in imperfect competition?

Chapter 5 Review (pp. 90-91)

Have students complete the Chapter Review. They may work in pairs or in small groups. Ask if there are any questions about the topics covered in this chapter.

Chapter Review Project (p. 91) Draw student's attention to the Chapter Review Project. Have students begin work on the project. Their goal for the first day is to decide on the product or service that the class corporation will provide and to fill out a charter application.

The following day, ask students to clarify any aspects of their charter application that are not clear. Grant the class its charter. Then have the class conduct elections for a three-person board of directors. The board of directors will then choose a CEO, vice presidents, and department heads. Then have the class work on an organizational chart for the company. Finally, have the groups share their charts with the class.

Cooperative Learning Activities

1. Have students work as groups of investors. Each group should choose three to five stocks in which to invest a total of $10,000. Ask the groups to record the number of stock shares bought and their total value based on a current newspaper listing. Then have the groups check the value of their stocks at the end of two weeks. Did they make or lose money?

2. Have students work in small groups to research a company of their choice. They will need help from the school or public librarian. They should find information on the history of the company; its organization, whether it is a sole proprietorship, partnership, or corporation; and its profit and loss record. Have students prepare and give an oral or visual presentation of their findings to the class.

Chapter 5 Test Answers

(1 point for 1-10; 2 points for 11-12; 3 points for 13-14)

1. c **2.** a **3.** b **4.** d **5.** c **6.** geographical monopoly **7.** government **8.** technological monopoly **9.** oligopoly **10.** price fixing **11.** Sole proprietorship is owned by one person who makes all the decisions and takes all the risks. A sole proprietor risks his or her own money and personal property. A general partnership is owned by two or more people who share the decision making and risks. A corporation is established by charter and is owned by stockholders who risk only what they invest. Decisions are made by a board of directors. **12.** Answers may vary. Many companies make aspirin, but Bayer had the best brand-name recognition and so had a lion's share of the aspirin market. Monopolistic competition occurs when one producer is perceived as far better or more desirable than the others. **13.** Answers may vary. Small businesses involve relatively smaller amounts of capital and smaller amounts of risk. Because the number of people involved is small, a complex organization is not necessary. A large company involves a great deal of capital and, therefore, much more risk. It needs organization to oversee all its employees and departments. **14.** Answers may vary. One producer buys out other producers so that it now is by far the largest seller. That producer can order parts more cheaply because of volume, and can afford to offer the product at a lower price, thereby lowering the price for everyone.

CHAPTER 5 TEST

Circle the letter of the best answer.

1. Which type of business needs a charter?
   a. sole proprietorship
   b. partnership
   c. corporation
   d. all businesses

2. The money that a business must pay for using the bank's money is called
   a. interest.
   b. profit.
   c. expense.
   d. loan.

3. Parts of the company owned by shareholders are called
   a. bonds.
   b. stocks.
   c. partnerships.
   d. charters.

4. Which form of business seems most risky for an individual?
   a. a small corporation
   b. a large corporation
   c. a partnership
   d. a sole proprietorship

5. If no single buyer or seller of a product can control the selling price, that product can be said to enjoy
   a. a monopoly.
   b. an oligopoly.
   c. perfect competition.
   d. monopolistic competition.

Complete each statement.

6. A _____ occurs when there is only one seller of a product in a certain area.

7. To control prices in a natural monopoly, the _____ makes rules about prices.

8. A _____ occurs when a person has a patent for his or her invention.

9. When a market is dominated by a few competitors, it is a(n) _____.

10. A secret, illegal agreement to keep prices high is called _____.

Answer the following.

11. Describe the three types of businesses.

_____
_____
_____
_____
_____

12. Give an example and/or description of monopolistic competition.

_____
_____
_____
_____
_____

13. Most small businesses are sole proprietorships. All large businesses are corporations. Why do you think this is so?

_____
_____
_____
_____
_____

14. Describe a change in circumstances that would alter the climate for a product from perfect competition to imperfect competition.

_____
_____
_____
_____
_____

Chapter 6: Labor and Pay

Motivation

Ask students to discuss the types of jobs that are open to them. What do students look for when choosing a part-time job? What skills do they have to offer the job market?

Then ask students how they look for jobs. Have they looked at want ads in newspapers? Have they ever interviewed for a job? Ask volunteers to share their experiences.

After this general discussion, have students brainstorm a list of jobs that do not require special skills or previous experience. Ask students which of these jobs would be more desirable if the pay per hour were the same for each.

A Worker's Strengths (pp. 92–95)

This case study focuses on issues of labor and pay. It presents categories of labor and discusses how pay relates to skills, how pay affects supply and demand, and how and why unions developed. The case study also covers payroll deductions in depth.

Have students read the case study. Ask them to pay attention to how Mitch Curren's job description and skills have changed over the course of her career at Ben & Jerry's.

Terms Covered labor force, white-collar workers, blue-collar workers, skill level, unskilled workers, semi-skilled workers, skilled workers, professionals, labor unions, discrimination, cost of living, gross pay, net pay, federal income tax, state income tax, FICA, Medicare tax, medical insurance, 401K, pay stub

Reading Comprehension After students have read the case study, ask the following reading comprehension questions. Encourage students to look back at the case study if they cannot answer a question.

1. What job did Mitch Curren have when she saw the Ben & Jerry's help-wanted ad? (Curren was a writing instructor at Vermont State College.)

2. Why was she looking at job ads? (Although Curren thought that her job as an instructor was good, it did not pay very well.)

3. What skills did Curren have that the people at Ben & Jerry's wanted? (The people at Ben & Jerry's were interested in Curren's speaking and communication skills.)

4. What was Curren's first job at Ben & Jerry's? (She was a tour guide.)

5. Was it the job that she expected to get? Explain. (No. Curren could not see herself as a tour guide. She was terrified at the idea of doing things that she had never done before.)

6. How did Curren learn what she needed to know as a tour guide? (She asked a lot of questions. She also went to "boot camp" where she learned about making ice cream.)

7. What job did Curren do in the public relations department? (Curren promoted Ben & Jerry's unusual business ideas.)

8. What is one of Ben & Jerry's unusual business ideas? (The company works to make a better world.)

9. Give some examples of how Ben & Jerry's carries out this idea. (The company donates profits to charity; tries to prevent industrial pollution; helps environmental groups; recycles; and orders ingredients from family-owned businesses and from companies that employ homeless and disadvantaged people)

10. How did Curren create her own job at Ben & Jerry's? (Because of Curren's communication skills, she was able to handle the thousands of telephone calls that Ben & Jerry's receives every year.)

11. What unusual methods does Curren use to get the word out about Ben & Jerry's? (She uses an on-line computer network. She also gives speeches, throws parties, and writes pamphlets.)

Learning and Applying Economics

Skilled and Unskilled Workers (pp. 96-100)
There are several ways of classifying workers. One way is to determine whether the jobs they do produce a good or a service. Begin a discussion by writing the categories "Produces a good" and "Provides a service" on the chalkboard. Have students brainstorm to list as many jobs as they can for each category.

Leave the lists on display. Have students read the sections titled "Skilled and Unskilled Workers" and "White-Collar and Blue-Collar Workers." Ask students to look at the chalkboard lists again and identify which of the jobs listed are white-collar and which are blue-collar. You might use *W* and *B* as codes next to each job. Then have students answer questions 1-4 independently.

Then direct students' attention to the chart on page 97 comparing white- and blue-collar jobs. Ask them to think of other examples and exceptions for each category. Discuss the answers to questions 5 and 6 as a class.

Take Another Look (p. 98) Have students work in pairs on questions 7-9 in the "Take Another Look" section. Point out that on a circle graph, the percentages must add up to 100.

Explain to students that another way of classifying jobs is by skill level. Have students work in small groups to read the "Skill Levels" section (page 99). Ask them to think of at least three more jobs for each skill level described. Have each group report to the class the jobs it listed in each category. Students can then work together to answer questions 10-12. Then have students work independently to answer questions 13-19 in the "Check Your Understanding" section on page 100.

Next, ask students to identify ways that workers acquire skills. Relate this idea to trade-offs, as discussed in Chapter 1. What trade-offs do workers make when acquiring job skills? What do they lose and what do they gain by acquiring job skills? An example would be professionals who attend more than four years of college. These workers usually have to take out school loans to finish their education. The trade-off for that debt is usually higher pay and better job security.

As a class, read and discuss "The Trouble with Categories." Have students answer question 20 as a class.

Supply and Demand in the Labor Market (pp. 100-103) Ask students to review the terms *supply* and *demand* and to discuss what these terms mean with respect to products and prices. Work with the class to define those same terms with respect to the labor market.

Point out that the labor supply is high for a given job at a given wage if there are many workers both able and willing to work for that wage. Similarly, the labor supply is low for a given job at a given wage if there are not many workers able to do that job, or if those workers are not willing to work at that wage.

Have students work in small groups to read and discuss "Supply and Demand in the Labor Market," "How Demand Affects Pay," and "How Supply Affects Pay." Have them work together to answer questions 21-24. Ask students to identify the sellers and buyers in the labor market.

Then tell students to read "Other Factors that Affect Pay" (page 102). Ask students to think of different examples of each of these factors. For example, other skills might be specialized knowledge of accounting or engineering. In terms of job types, many people would like to be extras in a movie and, therefore, would be willing to work for less. On the other hand, a stunt person in a movie takes physical risks and, therefore, gets higher pay. Other job location situations might involve public transportation and housing. A company in a remote area, or one in an area in which there is a shortage of housing, may have difficulty finding enough workers at a lower wage.

In the section "Demanding Higher Pay" (page 102), have students discuss current examples from professional sports.

Ask students to share any experiences that they have had in asking for and/or getting higher pay for a job. Then have students complete questions 25-27 for homework.

Labor Unions (pp. 103-104) Have students work together in small groups to read and discuss the sections "Labor Unions" and "Unions Gain Power" and to answer questions 28-30.

Ask each group to name as many labor unions (or jobs that have labor unions) as they can. For each, ask the group to list issues that they think would be of interest to that particular union.

Students may recall facts about the rise of unions from their study of U.S. history. They may know about the 1824 strike by weavers in Pawtuckett, Rhode Island, the first strike involving women. In 1877, President Rutherford B. Hayes sent troops to intervene in a violent railroad strike. In 1886, a Chicago labor rally protesting police action against strikers turned into the Haymarket Riot. You might wish to offer extra-credit projects researching the history of unions and their affect on supply and demand.

Multicultural Note

Since the early 1800's, workers had tried to organize unions to win better conditions. Most early efforts to form unions failed. Then, in 1869, workers formed a labor union called the Knights of Labor. The Knights was originally open to skilled workers only. Workers held secret meetings and greeted each other with special handshakes. Secrecy was necessary because employers fired workers who joined unions.

Ten years later, the Knights allowed women, African Americans, immigrants, and unskilled workers join.

The new union wanted shorter working hours, equal pay for men and women, and an end to child labor.

Think About It! (p. 105) As a class, read and discuss the "Think About It!" section. Help students recall what they learned about the Consumer Price Index in Chapter 4. Remind students that the Consumer Price Index compares average prices of selected goods and services in one year with those of an earlier, or base, year. This measure is often used to determine changes in the cost of living. Ask students to discuss how the Consumer Price Index might influence a minimum wage increase. Then have students answer questions 31-32.

Getting a Paycheck (pp. 105-106) Write on the chalkboard: "Gross pay - Deductions = Net Pay." Tell students that gross pay is the wage that the employer pays for that job. Taxes and other deductions are subtracted from the gross pay. The result is net pay, which is the money that the worker actually receives. Ask students to read about the types of deductions and to determine which are mandatory and which are not. Ask volunteers to explain each of the deductions listed. Discuss the specific state or local deductions for your community. Have students answer questions 33-35.

Using Economics Skills (p. 107)

Have students work in small groups to read and discuss the "Using Economics Skills" section and to answer questions 1-5.

Guided Discussion Topics

Use the following questions to focus students' attention on the chapter's main points.

- Curren got her training as a tour guide by actually making and serving ice cream. Was this training necessary? Explain.
- What skills do you think Curren brought to her job as Ben & Jerry's "Info Queen?"
- How has Curren's job description and salary changed during the years that she's worked at Ben & Jerry's?
- You saw that one way that jobs could be categorized is as white-collar or blue-collar. Another way is by skill level. Which way seems better? Why?
- Is this statement true or false: "White-collar workers usually make more money than blue-collar workers." Explain.
- State the law of supply for the labor market.
- State the law of demand for the labor market.
- What factors other than supply and demand can affect wages?
- Why do you think that the U.S. government usually sided with business in labor union matters before the early 1900s?
- Business groups and labor unions send lobbyists to talk with state and federal government representatives. Lobbyists are people who try to influence lawmakers to vote in a certain way. Lobbyists are paid by the organizations or companies that they represent. What government policies do you think are of interest to business groups, labor unions, and their lobbyists?

- Businesses want to increase profits. Unions want to increase pay. Is it in the labor unions' interest that a business stays profitable? Explain.
- Why do you think the government has mandated that taxes be withheld from wages?
- Why do you think companies offer benefits, such as retirement plans and health care?

Chapter 6 Review (pp. 108–109)

Have students complete the Chapter Review either independently or in pairs. Encourage them to ask questions about any concepts that remain unclear.

Chapter Review Project (p. 109) Form small groups to work on the Chapter Review Project. Have each group decide how it will gather a variety of want ads. Have them prepare a chart to use when analyzing the want ads. The charts should include job categories, such as retail, business, or education. Students can paste the ads under the appropriate headings and compare the skills and pay offered for each job.

After students have finished analyzing the want ads that they collected, have students give a 5-minute presentation of their findings.

Cooperative Learning Activity

Have the class choose a product or service of interest to them.

Form small groups of students. Tell half of the groups that they are employers that provide the product or service. Tell the other half that they are workers. Have each group of employers make a list of jobs that they need filled. For each job on the list, have them write a want ad. Each want ad should get a group letter and a number so that it is easy to identify.

Then each set of want ads should be read by each set of workers. One person in each group should keep count of how many workers are interested in each ad. Have each group report its tallies. Make a master list to which the whole class may refer. Discuss the master list in terms of the supply and demand of labor. Why were some jobs more appealing to prospective employees? Why were the other jobs less appealing?

Have the workers go on mock interviews for the jobs that interest them. Employers must decide as a group which traits and skills the job requires and which workers they will hire.

If there are jobs that are not filled, have that employer group rewrite the ad to try to attract more workers. Continue until all jobs are filled.

Chapter 6 Test Answers

(1 point for 1-10; 2 points for 11-12; 3 points for 13-14)

1. c **2.** d **3.** a **4.** c **5.** b **6.** Blue-collar **7.** Supply **8.** increases **9.** strike **10.** Medical insurance **11.** unskilled: little training or education, low pay; semi-skilled: some training or education, low to medium pay; skilled: special training and education, medium to high pay; professional: highly trained and educated, usually very high pay **12.** skill, job type, and job location **13.** Answers may vary. These categories cannot always predict levels of training, pay, or responsibility. Some white-collar workers, such as file clerks, have little training and do not earn high pay. Some blue-collar workers, such as carpenters and electricians, have a lot of training and skill and earn high pay. **14.** Answers may vary. If there are other builders in town, Leroy may be able to get a better-paying job with one of them, or he can renegotiate with his present boss. If there are few other employment opportunities in his community, Leroy may have to wait a few months and ask for a raise again. His family responsibilities may also affect whether he stays with that builder or tries to move to a new location.

CHAPTER 6 TEST

Circle the letter of the best answer.

1. The total number of people over age 16 who are working or looking for work is
   a. a labor union.
   b. an employee.
   c. the labor force.
   d. a professional.

2. Which of the following jobs is *not* a white-collar job?
   a. computer operator
   b. typist
   c. doctor
   d. carpenter

3. The willingness of a business to buy labor at a given price is
   a. demand.
   b. supply.
   c. wages.
   d. gross pay.

4. Groups of workers who band together are
   a. marketing departments.
   b. labor forces.
   c. labor unions.
   d. employees.

5. The total amount of money earned before deductions are subtracted is your
   a. salary.
   b. gross pay.
   c. net pay.
   d. union wage.

Complete each statement.

6. _____ workers include bus drivers, factory workers, miners, and plumbers.

7. _____ is the willingness of workers to sell their labor at given prices.

8. When employers offer high pay, the numbers of workers interested in a job _____.

9. Union workers stop working when their union calls a _____ in an effort to get employers to meet its demands.

10. _____ helps people under age 65 pay for their medical care.

Answer the following.

11. Name and describe the four skill levels of workers.

12. Name three factors other than supply and demand that affect pay.

13. Why are categories, such as white-collar and blue-collar, misleading?

14. Leroy works as a carpenter for a builder in a small town. The builder thinks well of Leroy's work. However, when Leroy asks for a raise, he doesn't get one. What options do you think Leroy has? What circumstances in his life and/or in his community may influence how he decides to act?

Chapter 7: Money and Banking

Motivation

Have students work in small groups to talk about credit cards. Ask them to share what they know about types of credit cards, how difficult or easy they are to get, and what they can purchase.

Ask each group to make a poster, or write a script for a public service announcement, called "Wise Use of Credit Cards." Ask students to include the advantages and disadvantages of using credit cards in the information on the poster or in the script.

To illusratate the disadvantages of credit cards, you might you the following example:

If you buy a stereo system for $1,000 on a credit card that charges 18% interest, and you make the minimum payments of $29.37 each month for four years (48 months), you will end up paying $1,409.76 for that stereo.

Sarah's Freedom from Credit Card Debt (pp. 110–113)

Using the example of a young person in deep credit card debt, this case study presents information about money, credit, banking, and the Federal Reserve System.

Have students read the case study. Ask them to pay attention to the descriptions of how money and credit are obtained and used.

Terms Covered barter, exchange, buying power, commodity money, fiat money, representative money, near money, divisible, currency, savings accounts, passbook accounts, certificates of deposit, banks, personal checks, traveler's checks, savings and loan associations, bank statement, government bonds, money supply, the Federal Reserve System

Reading Comprehension After students have read the case study, discuss it with them by asking the following reading comprehension questions. Encourage students to look back at the case study as the class discusses it.

1. How was Sarah affected by her living expenses after high school? (Sarah was surprised by her money troubles.)

2. What role did Sarah's parents play in helping her? (Her parents paid for Sarah's living expenses, college tuition, and car payments.)

3. What role did Sarah play? (Sarah's part-time job paid for clothes and entertainment expenses.)

4. What was one disadvantage of the financial help that Sarah's parents were able to give her? (Because money was never a problem, they did not teach Sarah about managing her finances.)

5. How did Sarah manage her money after college? (She began using her credit cards more and more.)

6. Did she have trouble with credit cards from the very beginning? Explain. (No. In the beginning, Sarah was able to make all her credit card payments. Later, however, she was unable to pay even the minimum balance on her cards.)

7. What was the difference for Sarah between the American Express card and the MasterCard? (The American Express card required Sarah to pay her balance in full; the MasterCard allowed her to carry a balance.)

8. How did this difference get her into trouble? (Sarah began carrying a larger and larger balance on her MasterCard and paid high finance charges to do so.)

9. What kind of help was Sarah able to get for her debt problems? (Sarah sought the help of a financial consultant.)

Learning and Applying Economics

Exchange, Money, and Interdependence (pp. 114–115) Explain the term *barter* as the direct trading of one good or service for another. Ask students to describe how barter may have worked in a small community before the invention of money. Ask them to describe what exchanges of goods and services might have taken place. Encourage all students to make some guesses.

Ask students to consider the following modern barter arrangement:

Owen wants to borrow his friend José's car for a day trip to the beach. He knows that José is painting his house. Owen offers to help José paint his house all day Saturday if José lets him borrow his car on Sunday.

Does this arrangement sound fair? What would make the arrangement acceptable to both parties? What could go wrong?

After this general discussion of a barter system, ask students to form small groups. Have them read and discuss the "Exchange, Money, and Interdependence" section and answer questions 1-4. Ask students to tell you the three functions of money and how each is an improvement over the barter system.

Characteristics of Money (pp. 115-120)
Ask students to imagine a society that has a great number of eggs, so many eggs that they are used as money. Ask students to make a list of advantages and disadvantages of using eggs as money. Then ask them to brainstorm as many adjectives as they can to describe a good that would be suitable for use as money.

In small groups, have students read the "Characteristics of Money" section. Have them answer questions 5-8 and work together on the "Check Your Understanding" section.

When students have completed the "Check Your Understanding" section, ask them to tell you how U.S. money fits the four characteristics of money.

In the same groups, ask students to read "Types of Money." Have them discuss and answer questions 9-12.

Take Another Look (p. 119) After students have completed the "Take Another Look" section, ask them to add these items to the chart and make the appropriate check marks: individual pearls, gift certificates, Japanese yen. Discuss why each of these are or are not examples of money.

Next, write on the chalkboard the three functions of money: "medium of exchange, unit of value, store of value." Then ask students if they are familiar with savings account passbooks. Have volunteers explain what passbooks look like and how they work. Ask students if savings account passbooks are money. Have them look at the three functions of money listed on the board and tell you which of the functions passbooks fulfill.

Then have students read the "Near Money" section (pp. 119-120). After students answer questions 13-15, you may want to point out that other examples of near money are government and corporate bonds. If you purchase government and corporate bonds, the corporation or government holds the bonds for a specific amount of time, after which you can cash in your bonds for a certain amount of money. You agree to let the government or corporation use the money until you cash in your bonds.

Multicultural Notes

- Lydia, a small country that existed in what is now western Turkey, may have first introduced coin money as a medium of exchange. It is believed the coins were made during the 600s B.C.E. Lydia's coins carried the imprint of its king's image to guarantee that the coins were the correct weight and value.

- In the 1200s, Italian trader Marco Polo was surprised to see that the Chinese used paper money instead of coins. China began using paper money in the 600s C.E., but it took the Europeans until the 1600s to adopt paper money.

- Cowrie shells, from sea snails, were once used as money in China, India, and Africa.

- The Inca, Indians who lived in Ancient Peru and had a complex civilization, did not use money. They often used cloth as a medium of exchange. The government controlled any trading of metals, precious stones, or unusual plants and animals.

Financial Institutions (pp. 120-121) Ask students to work in pairs or small groups to read the "Financial Institutions" section and answer questions 16-18. Have them discuss what they think the benefits might be of having an account in an S&L rather than a bank, or vice versa. Do they think that because an S&L is smaller, they might get better service? Why or why not? Give students about 15 minutes to discuss their positions.

Money Supply (pp. 121-122) Have students read the "Money Supply" section and answer questions 19-20. Then write two names on the chalkboard, Elena and Jill, for example, and tell students the following situation:

Elena received $50 for her birthday, and she loaned Jill $15 to buy a new CD. Now, Elena has only $35 and Jill has $15. The total is still $50.

Ask students how banks manage to expand the money supply by making loans. How is the loan situation with a bank different from the loan situation between the two friends? (The bank counts on the fact that depositors do not demand their money all at once. At any given time, the bank may not have every last cent that people have deposited with it.)

The Federal Reserve System (pp. 122-124) Tell students that control of the U.S. money supply is the responsibility of the Federal Reserve System. Then have students read and discuss the four main functions of the Federal Reserve System. Ask the class to discuss why it is necessary for the Federal Reserve System to handle these functions. What if the Federal Reserve System didn't regulate the U.S. banking system or supply currency? Have students answer questions 21-23 for homework.

Next, ask students to discuss any experiences that they have had with stores, banks, or mail-order companies that they believe cheated them out of money. For any situation presented, ask students whether (and if so how) the government could protect them in that situation. If students cannot think of any examples, tell them the following story about Joella, who had her bank card stolen.

Joella reported that her credit card was stolen the very day that it happened. The next month, her bank statement showed that someone had made a cash withdrawal of $400 five days after she had reported the card stolen.

Ask students if they think Joella should lose the $400. Ask them if they think that the bank should lose the $400. Ask them what they think will happen.

After this discussion of consumer problems, have students read the "Protecting the Consumer" section (page 124) and answer the "Check Your Understanding" questions.

Using Economics Skills (p. 125)

Have students work in small groups on this section. After students have read the text and answered questions 1-4, ask each group to write four more questions that could be answered using the same checking account statement. Then have each group give its questions to another group to answer. Do this until every group has answered every other group's questions.

Guided Discussion Topics

Use the following questions to focus students' attention on the chapter's main points.

- How did Sarah get into so much debt?
- How was Sarah able to get out of debt?
- How do you think parents can best prepare their children for managing money?
- Why do you think store owners accept credit cards knowing that they will not get their money immediately?
- Why do you think banks offer credit cards to people who do not ask for them?
- Before money was invented, how did people get items that they needed?
- Why are credit cards not considered a form of money?
- Give the pros and cons of using small pebbles as money.
- Why do Certificates of Deposit often earn higher interest if the time of deposit is longer?
- Why is a savings account passbook not considered money?
- Why is the interest on a credit card balance often greater than on a bank loan?
- How many main Federal Reserve Banks are there?
- Why do you think it is important for the government to have laws that protect consumers?

Chapter 7 Review (pp. 126-127)

Have students complete the Chapter Review questions and ask about any points that they do not understand.

Chapter Review Project (p. 127)

Start the Chapter Review Project by brainstorming with students on the list of what to look for when choosing a bank. Have students name four or five banks in their area. Form groups of students to research each bank. Students in each group should decide how they are going to get the information from their bank and how they will present their findings.

Have the groups finalize work on their project. Give each group time to present the information it gathered about its bank. Then have the whole class discuss which bank seems to offer the best services.

Cooperative Learning Activity

Have students form into groups of three or four. Give each group 10 index cards, or small pieces of paper. On each slip of paper, the groups will write a checkbook entry for a fictitious person. For example: December 5, deposit $125, or December 6, Check #203 to Telephone Company for $52.18. At least one card must say "Opening Balance" and give some agreed upon amount of money. (Each person in the group should write at least two cards.) When the group has completed 10 cards, have one student write on a sheet of paper, "These are the checking account transactions of (made-up name)." Have each group deliver its 10 cards and the sheet of paper to another group. Now, each group takes the stack of cards it has received and completes a checking account record for the fictitious person. Students should start with the "Opening Balance" card and record the rest of the cards in order by date. For each new entry, they should compute the new balance. One member of the group should be responsible for rechecking all of the arithmetic.

Chapter 7 Test Answers

(1 point for 1-10; 2 points for 11-12; 3 points for 13-14)

1. b **2.** c **3.** d **4.** a **5.** d **6.** Barter **7.** portable **8.** representative **9.** savings and loan association **10.** Federal Reserve System **11.** medium of exchange, unit of value, store of value **12.** oversee and regulate U.S. banks, supply currency, clear checks, control the U.S. money supply **13.** Banks take money that depositors have left with them and lend it to others. The depositor still has money in the bank earning interest and the borrower has more money than he or she had before. For example, if a depositor has $4,000 in the bank and the bank lends $1,000 to someone else, there is now $5,000 total in use. **14.** The Truth in Lending Act requires lending institutions to inform borrowers fully about their loan details. Lenders must tell borrowers their exact interest rate and repayment schedule. The Equal Credit Opportunity Act states that lenders must make decisions about credit on the same basis for all applicants of similar economic condition. They cannot treat applicants differently because of gender, ethnicity, age, marital status, or national origin. The Electronic Funds Transfer Act states that a consumer who reports a bank card missing within two days is responsible for no more than $50 in losses if someone uses that bank card illegally.

CHAPTER 7 TEST

Circle the letter of the best answer.

1. Money that is itself valuable is
   a. a barter system.
   b. commodity money.
   c. fiat money.
   d. representative money.

2. Money made valuable by government order is
   a. a tax.
   b. commodity money.
   c. fiat money.
   d. representative money.

3. Money paid for the use of someone else's money is
   a. a tax.
   b. fiat.
   c. barter.
   d. interest.

4. The total value of currency and checkable deposits in the U.S. economy is
   a. the money supply.
   b. interest.
   c. an exchange.
   d. The Fed.

5. A savings account passbook is an example of
   a. representative money.
   b. fiat money.
   c. commodity money.
   d. near money.

Complete each sentence.

6. _____ is the direct trading of one good or service for another.

7. Money is _____, which means that it is easy to carry from place to place.

8. Personal checks are an example of _____ money.

9. A _____ is an institution that accepts savings deposits and makes loans, usually to people who want to buy homes.

10. Control of the U.S. money supply is the responsibility of the _____.

Answer the following.

11. Name the three functions of money.

12. Name the four functions of the Federal Reserve.

13. Describe how banks are able to expand the money supply.

14. Describe how these three laws affect consumers: Truth in Lending Act, Equal Credit Opportunity Act, and Electronic Funds Transfer Act.

Chapter 8: Investments and Your Future

Motivation

Ask students if they know anyone who is retired. Have them tell what they know about how retired people pay their living expenses. Students may mention savings accounts and pensions. Have students review what they learned about Social Security benefits and 401Ks in Chapter 6.

Ask students to imagine someone who saves $50 every month from the time he or she is 20 years old until he or she is age 65. Have students help you determine that, to find out the total amount of money saved, you must multiply $50 by 12 months by 45 years. The result is $27,000 (without interest). Now talk about interest (remind students what they learned about interest in Chapter 5). Show students the "Power of Compounding" chart below and point out that at 5 percent annual interest that $27,000 would become $101,744.04 after 45 years. Talk about how much further that extra $74,744.04 would go in retirement. Tell students that this chapter will teach them about ways of investing their money to make it grow faster.

The Power of Compounding

The following table compares a $50-a-month investment earning no interest and one earning 5 percent annual interest (compounded monthly on the first of each month for 45 years).

Years	0% Interest	5% Interest
5	$3,000	3,414.47
10	$6,000	$7,796.46
15	$9,000	$13,420.13
20	$12,000	$20,637.32
25	$15,000	$29,899.55
30	$18,000	$41,786.32
35	$21,000	$57,041.31
40	$24,000	$76,618.93
45	$27,000	$101,744.04

Investing in Yourself First
(pp. 128–130)

In this case study, students are introduced to types of investments, including stocks and bonds.

Have students read the case study. Encourage them to write down new vocabulary words as they read them.

Terms Covered investment, securities, mutual funds, U.S. savings bonds, speculation, capital gains, common stock, preferred stock, capital loss, stock split, broker, stock exchanges, general mutual funds, sector mutual funds, Dow Jones Industrial Average, bear market, bull market, money market mutual fund

Reading Comprehension Discuss the case study as a class. Ask students to read you any new vocabulary words that they wrote down as they read the case study. Write these vocabulary words on the chalkboard and be sure to refer to them in the course of the discussion. Then ask the following reading comprehension questions. Encourage students to look back at the case study if they can't answer a question.

1. About how old is Lucas? (He just graduated college with a bachelor's degree, so he is about 22.)

2. Why is Lucas talking to Mr. Melendez, the personnel manager at Nortec? (Lucas is talking to him to learn about Nortec's benefits package.)

3. What decisions did Lucas have to make about the company's retirement plan? (Lucas had to decide which mutual fund he wanted to invest in—stocks or bonds.)

4. What did Mr. Melendez point out to Lucas about the value of saving $50 a month at 10 percent interest a year after 10 years? after 20 years? after 30 years? (Mr. Melendez pointed out that a $50-a-month investment paying 10 percent interest compounded monthly will do more than just double between 10 and 20, or 20

and 40 years. A $50-a-month investment at 10 percent interest will grow to $10,327.60 in 10 years, $38,284.85 in 20 years, and $113,966.27 in 30 years.)

5. How does this savings compare with the actual amount of money saved without interest? (After 10 years, the amount saved is $6,000, after 20 years it is $12,000, and after 30 years it is $18,000. Comparing these figures will help students see how dramatic a difference investment returns can make.)

6. What types of mutual funds did Mr. Melendez describe to Lucas? (He described stock-based and bond-based mutual funds.)

7. What did Mr. Melendez say was the difference between the types? (Bonds are a loan of sorts, and stocks are part ownership of a corporation. Bonds are safer but, on average, don't earn as much as stocks. Stocks earn more, but they are riskier.)

8. What did Lucas decide, and why did he make that decision? (Lucas chose stocks because at his age he would have time to make up any losses his riskier stock investments might incur.)

Multicultural Note

In a global economy, investors are interested in stocks from other countries, as well as their own. *The New York Times* lists stock prices from 24 countries, as well as 20 different stock indexes. The indexes are in Canada, Mexico, South America, Australia, Europe, Africa, and Asia.

Learning and Applying Economics

Stocks and Bonds/Starting an Investment Program (pp. 131-133) Discuss the word *investment* and its meanings with the class. Explain how investing usually means buying or doing something that will have a future payoff. Use the following examples to illustrate your point. A student might say, "I am going to practice my word processing skills. It's an investment in increasing my chances of getting a good part-time job." A teenager might say, "I bought a leaf blower last year. Now, I get a lot of work cleaning up yards for people in my neighborhood. It was a good investment." Ask students to come up with their own examples of investments. Discuss these and other uses of the word *investment*.

Then explain to students that in this lesson investment refers to putting money in securities with the idea of making some profit on the money for use in the future.

Have students work in small groups to read the "Stocks and Bonds" and "Starting an Investment Program" sections. Have students discuss and answer questions 1-8.

When the students have finished, ask them to summarize the types of bonds described in the section.

Stocks (pp. 133-136) Remind students that they learned about stocks and stockholders in Chapter 5. Ask them to define *stocks* and explain how stockholders influence a corporation. (They elect a board of directors that chooses the CEO.) Ask students to describe how the increase or decrease in the profits of the company may affect the value of the stock.

Explain that the value of a stock may increase tremendously if the company does extremely well. For example, a company that develops a new product that is quite successful may have its stock double or triple in a short period of time. This is why people are attracted to stock investments.

Write these terms on the chalkboard: *speculation*, *capital gains*, and *dividends* (defined in Chapter 5), *common stock*, *preferred stock*, *capital loss*, and *stock split*. Ask students to work in small groups to read pages 133-135 and find the definitions of these terms. After they have worked on the definitions for 30 minutes or so, ask volunteers to state in their own words the meaning of each of the terms.

Have students read the "Buying and Selling Stocks" section. Ask volunteers to tell about their experiences visiting a stock exchange. Ask students to answer questions 9-16. For homework, have students read the "Check Your Understanding" section and answer questions 17-18.

Mutual Funds (pp. 137-139) Have students read the "Mutual Funds," "Take Another Look," and "Types of Mutual Funds" sections. Have them work in small groups to discuss the types of mutual funds that are described in the sections and to answer questions 19-21. Then have each group make a list of stocks and/or bonds they would put in a general mutual fund if they were in charge of starting up a new mutual fund. Groups can then compare stocks, bonds, and companies on their lists and discuss their choices.

Give each group time to present its list to the class. Have the class discuss the pros and cons of having each security in a general mutual fund.

Then have students work in small groups to read the "Investing in Mutual Funds" section and answer questions 22-23.

Take Another Look (p. 139) You might suggest that students use calculators to answer questions 24 and 25. Direct students' attention to the chart. On the chalkboard, write "Nike up 3 percent, Urban Outfitters down 6 percent." Ask students to look at the chart and tell you what they think the overall effect of these two changes would be on the total dollar value of this mutual fund. [The Nike stock increases in value to $2,304,625, which is a gain of $67,125 (multiply $2,237,500 x 0.03). Urban Outfitters stocks would decrease in value to $827,200, which is a loss of $52,800 (multiply 880,000 x 0.06). The net change for the mutual fund is +$14,325 ($67,125 - $52,800 = $14,325).] Ask students to discuss how other possible combinations of upturns and downturns would affect the stock value and, therefore, the total dollar value of the mutual fund.

Then have students complete questions 24-25.

Investing in Stocks (pp. 140-141) Remind students that, at the end of the case study, Lucas decides to invest in some stocks on his own. Ask students what they think Lucas should consider when buying stocks. How can Lucas be sure that he is making good choices? Have students read "Investing in Stocks" and answer questions 26-28.

Think About It! (p. 141) Draw students' attention to the stock table. Make sure that they understand what each column heading means. You might compute on the board the value of 100 shares of Netscape at the last price (100 x $81.50 = $8,150). Then ask: "If Lucas owns 100 shares of this stock, and after five years it is worth $105 a share, how much will his total investment be worth? (100 x $105 = $10,500). As a class, answer questions 29-32.

Investing in Yourself (p. 142) Have students work in small groups to read "Investing in Yourself." Ask each group to talk about the similarities and differences between the two circle graphs in the "Take Another Look" section. After the groups have had time to discuss the graphs, ask each group to share its impressions of the two retirement strategies.

You may want to show students how these two strategies would be implemented for a given amount of money. For example, a total investment of $5,000 would be broken down as follows, according to the circle graph for a 25-year-old investor: $2,000 in large company stocks funds ($5,000 x 0.40), $1,500 in international stock funds ($5,000 x 0.30), $1,250 in small company stock funds ($5,000 x 0.25), and $250 ($5,000 x 0.05)in bonds. The same total investment, $5,000, would be broken down as follows, according to the circle graph for a 45-year-old investor: $1,750 in large company stock funds, $1,000 in small company stock funds, $1,000 in international stock funds, and $1,250 in bonds. Seeing the actual numbers should help students make the comparisons. Ask all students to write an answer to question 33.

Using Economics Skills (p. 143)

Have students work in pairs on this page. Make sure that they understand the labels and scale of the graph. Have them answer questions 1-3.

For homework, ask students to look for examples of double-line graphs in newspapers or magazines. Each student should bring in a copy of one graph and make up three questions that can be answered using the graph. Have students exchange graphs and questions to help hone their graph-reading skills.

Guided Discussion Topics

Use these questions to focus students' attention on the chapter's main points.

- Why should young people plan for retirement?
- Why would a young person's investment strategy be different from a middle-aged person's strategy?

- What investment choices do people have?
- How are mutual funds different from individual stocks and/or bonds?
- Why do you think some people buy high-risk stocks?
- Many investment firms give the advice, "Diversify!" What does this term mean?
- In chapter 7, you learned about how the federal government controls the money supply. Explain the effect on the money supply if the federal government issues bonds at a high interest rate.
- What information would you try to find out about a company before buying its stock?
- What investment strategy do you think is best for you? Explain.
- How and where are stocks bought and sold?
- Which companies do you think might be wise long-term investment choices?

Chapter 8 Review (pp. 144–145)

Have students work in small groups to complete the Chapter Review questions. Encourage them to ask questions about any concepts that remain unclear.

Chapter Review Project (p. 145) Divide the class into small groups. Have each group begin the Chapter Review Project by choosing two stocks to investigate. Ask them to decide where and how they will find out about the stocks. Have the groups discuss the two stocks each investigated and choose one as the best investment. Then have them work out the details of how they will keep track of the changes in value of both stocks over a time period that you choose. Each group must write a report or make a display, including a graph, showing how the values of the stocks change over time. The report or display should state whether the group believes it made the correct investment choice.

Cooperative Learning Activity

Have students form small investor groups and name their firms. Each group should have a newspaper that lists stock and bond prices. Each group should also have a calculator. Have each group decide how it wants to invest $100,000. The groups must agree on and record exactly how many shares of stock and/or bonds they will purchase for their portfolios. After the groups have decided which stocks and/or bonds they will purchase, ask volunteers from each group to explain what investments their group chose and why.

Have students monitor their securities throughout the year and award a certificate to the group that gets the most return on its investment. You might also want to keep a graph that charts the groups' progress monthly.

Chapter 8 Test Answers

(1 point for 1-10; 2 points for 11-12; 3 points for 13-14)

1. c **2.** a **3.** b **4.** c **5.** d **6.** stock split **7.** Common **8.** U.S. Savings Bond **9.** bonds **10.** capital gain **11.** bonds, stocks, mutual funds **12.** In a bear market, stock prices are generally declining; in a bull market, stock prices are generally increasing. **13.** Small company stocks are riskier. They may do very well but they also have a greater chance of not performing. Large company stocks are more stable and less risky. **14.** If an investment will be long-term, with time to recoup any losses, the advice is usually to invest more in stocks because they usually increase at a faster rate than bonds but may be riskier. If an investment will be short-term, the advice is more cautious: Buy more bonds because there is little risk of losing money.

CHAPTER 8 TEST

Circle the letter of the best answer.

1. Another name for stocks and bonds is
   a. shares.
   b. notes.
   c. securities.
   d. money.

2. Which type of mutual fund specializes in stocks in the same area of business?
   a. sector
   b. NASDAQ
   c. general
   d. preferred

3. Which type of stock always pays a dividend?
   a. common
   b. preferred
   c. sector
   d. mutual

4. The place where a stock of a particular company can be bought and sold is
   a. a bank.
   b. a government office.
   c. a stock exchange.
   d. the company itself.

5. All trading on this exchange is electronic.
   a. New York Stock Exchange
   b. American Stock Exchange
   c. The Fed
   d. NASDAQ

Complete each statement.

6. In a _____, stockholders get two or more shares for every one share they own.

7. _____ stocks may or may not pay dividends.

8. A _____ is purchased for less than its face value. The government promises to pay the face value after a certain number of years.

9. Usually, _____ are a less risky investment than stocks.

10. The profit made on an investment is called a _____.

Answer the following.

11. Name three types of investments.

12. What is the difference between a bear and a bull market?

13. Describe the difference in risk between a small company stock mutual fund and a large company stock mutual fund.

14. How is investment advice different for long-term investments than for short-term investments?

Chapter 9: Consumers and Economic Decision Making

Motivation

Ask students to talk about a recent purchase that they have made. How did they decide on the brand, type, or model of the product? Were they happy with their purchase? Why or why not?

Then ask students to discuss what steps they would take to buy a new color television. There are many brands, sizes, and features of color televisions. There are many stores that sell televisions. How would students decide where to shop and which television to buy?

Have students name ways that they can gather product information before purchasing the television. List the students' answers on the chalkboard. Encourage students to think of different information sources.

Start another list for places to buy electronic equipment. For each store listed, students should name advantages or disadvantages of buying at that type of store.

Max Comparison Shops (pp. 146–149)

In this case study, students are shown how consumers make decisions and how they can learn to be smarter shoppers. Students will learn about consumer rights and how to handle consumer complaints. The "Using Economic Skills" page teaches students how to get information from consumer magazines.

Have students read the case study. Ask them to pay attention to what Max learns about comparison shopping.

Terms Covered necessities, non-necessities or luxuries, budget, comparison shopping, consumer rights, unfair business practice, bait-and-switch

Reading Comprehension After students have read the case study, review the important points in a class discussion. Talk about the importance of asking the right questions when making a purchase and go over which questions to ask. Discuss consumer rights and consumer complaints. Then ask students the following reading comprehension questions. Encourage them to look back at the case study if they cannot answer a question.

1. Whom did Max ask about where to shop for a cassette player? (Max asked his sister Lucy.)

2. Where did Max first look for Jenny's present? (He went to Giant Electronics.)

3. Why did he decide not to buy the present at that store? (Max thought that the salesperson did not give him enough information about all the available models. The salesperson was also pushing Max to purchase the most expensive model.)

4. Where did Max go next? (Max then went to George's Radio Shop.)

5. Why didn't Max buy the present right away at George's Radio Shop? (George suggested that Max research personal cassette players in a consumer magazine.)

6. How did Max educate himself about portable cassette players? (He read the article that George gave him and decided exactly which features he definitely wanted.)

7. Where did Max finally buy Jenny's present? (Even though the prices were lower at Giant Electronics, Max bought Jenny's present at George's Radio Shop.)

8. Do you think that Max made the right decision? Explain. (Answers will vary. Some students will agree that Max made the right decision; others will disagree, saying that Max should have opted to go to the store that offered the lower price.)

Learning and Applying Economics

Buying: Deciding Whether to Buy (pp. 150–151) Remind students that in Chapter 1, they learned to make a distinction between wants and needs, or non-necessities and necessities. Explain that sometimes we buy what we need, and sometimes we buy what we want but do not actually need. Ask students to make lists of goods and services on which they spent money in the last week. Each student should indicate on his or her list which items were wants and which were needs.

Have students work in small groups to read "Luxuries vs. Necessities" and "What Consumers Buy." Then have them discuss and answer questions 1-4.

As a class, read and discuss "Buying: Deciding Whether to Buy." Have students answer questions 5-6.

Take Another Look (p. 152) Direct students' attention to the chart. Have students follow the decision path for different items. Ask volunteers to give examples of situations that would end in a "Buy It!" decision and situations that would end in a "Don't Buy!" decision. Then ask students to think of situations that would end in a "Probably Shouldn't Buy" statement. Ask them to describe how they would make the final decision in each situation.

Then have students answer questions 7-9 for homework.

Making a Budget (p. 153) Remind students that the question "Can I afford to buy it?" is one of two key questions to ask themselves before making a purchase. Ask students: "How do you know if you can afford a purchase? How do you know you will have enough money for the items that you really need?"

Have students work in small groups on the "Making a Budget" and "Think About It" sections. Have them answer question 10 and then discuss ways Max could rework his budget to save the money that he needs to buy Jenny's present (question 11). Students should decide if Max can save the money in one week, or if he will need more than one week. They should be sure that Max will have enough money for budget items that he really needs. Give each group five minutes to present its reworked budget to the class.

Ask each student to make his or her own budget based on earnings and/or allowance and wants and needs. Students do not have to share this information. Alternately, you could ask students to make a budget based on $25 per week and their expenses.

Being an Informed Consumer (pp. 154-156) On the chalkboard, write "Sources of Product Information." Have students brainstorm a list of information sources. Write students' suggestions on the chalkboard. Ask the class to look back over the list and classify similar sources. Discuss the pros and cons of each source.

Next, have students work in small groups to read and discuss "Being an Informed Consumer," "Comparison Shopping," and "Buying: Which One?" Have them answer questions 12-18.

Then ask each group to make a flow chart that lists the steps a consumer should take to get the best product at the best price. You may wish to place the flow charts on display, either in the classroom or in a central place in the school.

Consumer Rights (p. 156) Ask students to relate any purchasing experiences they have had during which they believed that they had been deceived in some way. They may have paid too much, been lied to about features, or the item itself may have been faulty in some way.

Have students read the "Consumer Rights" section and answer questions 19-20. As a class, discuss why each of the rights is important and give examples of what might happen if that particular right were absent. Ask students if they can think of any other rights consumers should have that are not listed here.

Then ask students what they would do if they got home with a purchase and found that it did not work properly. Elicit as many different responses as you can. Have the class read "Consumer Complaints: Taking Action" and answer questions 21-22.

Next, ask volunteers to do some role playing. Have one student be the consumer with a complaint, another be the store clerk, and another be the store manager. Have different trios of students demonstrate ways to resolve the problem by following the advice in the worktext. You may wish to have at least one group demonstrate what *not* to do.

Consumer Complaints (pp. 157-159) Note: For this session, bring in copies of *Consumer Research* and *Consumer Reports* magazines to circulate around the classroom.

Begin a discussion by asking students what they think they can do if a consumer complaint is not resolved by the seller.

Then divide the class into three groups to report on each of these types of agencies: better business bureaus, trade associations, and consumer groups. Give the "consumer groups" students copies of the consumer magazines that you brought to class. After reading "Consumer Complaints: Private Organizations," ask each group to write a description of its organization, what it does, and how it helps consumers. Have each group read its report to the class. After the presentations, have students complete question 23.

For homework, ask students to read "Consumer Complaints: Local and State Agencies" and answer questions 24-25. As part of their homework, ask them to find out the names of local and state consumer agencies in their community. (Direct students to a local library and/or telephone book for help.) Ask students to share their information in class the next day *or* have students write a brief report as part of their homework.

Multicultural Note

Sometimes the term *ombudsman* is used to describe a person whose job is resolving consumer complaints. The origin of this word is Swedish. *Ombudsman* means "representative." In Sweden and New Zealand, an ombudsman is a government official appointed to receive and investigate complaints of public abuses against private citizens. In this country, it may also be used to refer to anyone who investigates a complaint, including a consumer complaint, against a larger entity.

Consumer Complaints (pp. 159-160) Ask students to summarize what they have learned about consumer agencies. Have them list the private, local, and state agencies that they have studied. Then tell students that there are many consumer agencies that are part of the federal government. Have them read "Consumer Complaints: Federal Agencies" and answer question 26.

Next, ask students what they think a person could do if no agencies were able to help resolve a consumer problem. They will probably suggest that the consumer "go to court." Ask students to read the section titled "Consumer Complaints: Legal Action." Have them work in pairs to answer questions 27-28 and the "Check Your Understanding" questions 29-30. Students can share their answers for questions 29 and 30 in a class discussion.

Consumer Responsibility (p. 160) Have students read the "Consumer Responsibility" section. Ask small groups of students to make up two fictional consumer situations, one in which the consumer has a legitimate complaint and one in which the consumer does not. Ask the groups to share their consumer stories and to discuss consumer responsibility. Then have students answer question 31 as a class, with everyone suggesting additions and refinements for the list of responsibilities.

Using Economics Skills (p. 161)

This page shows students how to read a chart in a consumer magazine. These charts contain a great deal of information. Have students read the column headings to see which features are rated in this report. After students have answered questions 1-5, ask them to make up similar questions based on the same chart. Have them exchange and answer each other's questions

Guided Discussion Topics

Use the following questions to focus students' attention on the chapter's main points.

- Why did Max expect to get a good deal at a large electronics store?
- How were the motivations of Max and the salesperson at Giant Electronics different?
- How can you tell if something that you want to buy is a necessity or non-necessity?
- What is a budget? How do you make a budget?
- Why is it a good idea to get product information before making a purchase?
- After you have decided which type and brand of product you want, how can you find the best price?
- What is the first step you should take if you are not happy with a purchase?
- What can you do if the store does not resolve a consumer complaint?
- At what point in a consumer dispute would you go to court?
- In Chapter 1, you learned about trade-offs. How does doing research before you purchase a product involve a trade-off?

Chapter 9 Review
(pp. 162-163)

Assign the Chapter Review for students to work on in small groups. Encourage them to ask questions about any material in the lesson that they did not fully understand.

Have students complete the Chapter Review questions and the ratings of their chosen products. Each group should prepare a ratings sheet, summarizing its results, and present it to the class.

Chapter Review Project
(p. 167)

Have students work on the Chapter Review Project in small groups. Each group should decide on a product and work out the details of what brands and features they will rate. They should divide the work of obtaining the samples and any equipment that they will need for testing. Then have groups present their findings to the class.

Chapter 9 Test Answers

(1 point for 1-10; 2 points for 11-12; 3 points for 13-14)

1. d **2.** b **3.** c **4.** a **5.** c **6.** "Do I need it?" and "Can I afford it?" **7.** comparison shopping **8.** consumer rights **9.** *Consumer Reports* **10.** John F. Kennedy **11.** safety, information, choice, hearing, repayment **12.** Answers may vary. The Consumer's Union helps consumers solve problems and helps to pass laws to protect consumers. Consumer Product Safety Commission drafts regulations and makes rulings that prevent dangerous products from being sold. **13.** No. Getting the best price is not a consumer right; it is the responsibility of the consumer. **14.** "Bait-and-switch" occurs when a store advertises an item at a great price, then says that the item is no longer available but offers a similar product that is more expensive. This is unfair if the store had no intention of selling the original item at the advertised price and intentionally misled you.

Cooperative Learning Activities

1. Ask small groups of students to decide on a purchase that they want to make. Each group can then gather information from different sources about the product and, based on their findings, decide whether to make the purchase. When students have finished, have them share their information with each other.

2. Have small groups of students write a consumer guide brochure that could be distributed throughout the school. Each group should decide what information to include, the design, layout, and how the brochure might be distributed. Limit each group to one sheet of paper for the finished brochure. When students have completed the assignment, they should circulate their group's brochure among the other groups for comments. Students should then vote on which brochure should be distributed throughout the school.

CHAPTER 9 TEST

Circle the letter of the best answer.

1. People who buy goods and services to satisfy their wants and needs are
   a. citizens.
   b. producers.
   c. smart shoppers.
   d. consumers.

2. A ticket to a movie is an example of a
   a. necessity.
   b. non-necessity.
   c. product.
   d. service.

3. A plan for spending money over a specific period of time is called a
   a. spreadsheet.
   b. tax statement.
   c. budget.
   d. bank statement.

4. A private agency that provides consumer information and monitors advertising and selling practices is the
   a. Better Business Bureau.
   b. U.S. Office of Consumer Affairs.
   c. Consumer's Union.
   d. Consumer's Research Inc.

5. Small claims courts can handle a consumer claim if
   a. the store is local.
   b. the store is small.
   c. the money involved is less than a certain amount.
   d. the consumer does not want to use a lawyer.

Complete each statement.

6. The two questions that consumers should ask themselves before making a purchase are _____.

7. Checking prices on the same item in several different stores is called _____.

8. Safety, information, and choice are examples of U.S. _____.

9. One magazine that rates products is _____.

10. In 1962, President _____ outlined a bill of rights for consumers.

Answer the following.

11. What are the five consumer rights?

   _____
   _____
   _____
   _____
   _____

12. List two agencies that help consumers and tell how they can help.

   _____
   _____
   _____
   _____
   _____

13. Suppose you bought a car without air-conditioning for $10,000. You find that the same car with air-conditioning is sold at another dealership for $9,000. Do you have the right to get some money back from the dealer who sold you the car? Explain why or why not.

   _____
   _____
   _____
   _____
   _____

14. Describe "bait-and-switch." Tell why it is an unfair business practice.

   _____
   _____
   _____
   _____
   _____
   _____
   _____

Chapter 10: Global Economy

Motivation

Ask students to tell what they know about The Coca-Cola Company. In how many countries worldwide do they think Coca-Cola is sold? What other U. S. products do they think are sold worldwide? Then ask students what they know about products from other countries that are sold in the United States.

Divide students into small groups. Then have them generate a list of products that they know are made in the United States. For each product, ask them to think of reasons why people in other countries might want to buy the U.S. product. Then ask the groups to list products that they know are made in other countries. For each product, ask them to think of reasons why Americans might buy the imported product. Have students keep their lists for use in the Chapter Review.

Coca-Cola Expands Worldwide (pp. 164–167)

Assign the case study as independent reading. Using Coca-Cola as an example, this case study highlights many global economic issues, including: trade, multinational corporations, barriers to trade, and trade agreements.

Terms Covered international trade, specialization, market share, exports, imports, absolute advantage, comparative advantage, fixed exchange rate, flexible exchange rate, multinational corporations, subsidiaries, free trade, infant industry, tariffs, quotas, embargoes, North American Free Trade Agreement (NAFTA), and General Agreement on Tariffs and Trade (GATT)

Reading Comprehension After students have read the case study, focus on its key points by asking the following reading comprehension questions. Encourage students to look back at the case study for answers.

1. How did Coca-Cola start? (A pharmacist made the first batch of Coca-Cola syrup in his backyard in 1886. The syrup was then mixed with soda water and sold out of an Atlanta pharmacy for 5 cents a glass.)

2. When did Coca-Cola begin looking to expand to foreign markets? (The soft drink was first exported to Canada and Europe in the early 1900s, but the real push for foreign expansion came in 1923 when Coca-Cola's Foreign Department was established.)

3. How did World War II affect the growth of Coca-Cola? (By making sure U.S. servicemen could get Coke overseas, the company created new foreign customers.)

4. How does Coca-Cola create demand in foreign countries? (It creates demand through advertising.)

5. How was advertising for Diet Coke different in the United States and foreign markets? (The U.S. ad campaign focused on taste; the foreign market ad campaigns focused on calories.)

6. How do other countries get Coca-Cola? (Foreign markets get Coca-Cola that is bottled in their own countries.)

7. What features of its advertising account for Coca-Cola's success? (Coca-Cola's success hinges on its brand-name and trademark recognition, use of famous talent for its campaigns, and sponsorship of the Olympics.)

8. How have political changes in the world affected Coca-Cola sales? (Coca-Cola is always one of the first multinational corporations to move into a country previously closed to outside products. It has recently started selling in Vietnam, China, Russia, and former East Germany.)

9. What percentage of Coca-Cola's profits come from foreign markets? (80 percent)

10. If you had bought one share of Coca-Cola stock in 1919 for $40, how much would it be worth today? ($2.5 million)

Learning and Applying Economics

International Trade (pp. 168–170) Trade among nations is one of the oldest patterns of contact among peoples. Ask students to brainstorm a list of ways that international trade benefits all parties. Encourage students to consider byproducts, such as mutual understanding and tolerance, as well as economic benefits, such as variety of goods.

You might wish to illustrate the pros and cons of interntional trade with the following examples:

A. *Marco Polo traveled various parts of Asia to trade goods. He was able to bring back to Europe information about the peoples he encountered, as well as about the goods that could be purchased.*

B. *The Aztec Indians were the dominant civilization of central Mexico at the time of the Spanish invasion in 1519. The Spanish military leader Cortés relied heavily on the enemies of the Aztecs to conquer them. The Spaniards were interested in the wealth of the Aztecs, including their gold. The Aztec people were completely wiped out as a result of war and the diseases brought to their lands by the Europeans.*

Ask students which example illustrates the pros of international trade and which one illustrates the cons. Then have volunteers summarize the lessons to be learned about the pros and cons of international trade.

Next, have students read the "International Trade" and "Why International Trade?" sections and ask them to answer questions 1-6 independently. Have them identify products they purchase that come from foreign markets.

Take Another Look (p. 170) Ask students to describe how they think someone in the United States might have been able to sell scissors to people in France in 1850—before telephones, airplanes, fax machines, and computers. Then have them discuss how each of these technological innovations helped international trade.

Remind students that the market share of a company is the percentage of a market controlled by that company. Point out again that the market share of Japanese cars increased dramatically in the 1970s because Japanese cars were more fuel efficient than American cars.

Direct students' attention to the pie graph. As students answers question 7, point out that the graph illustrates the American soft drink market, not the world's soft-drink market. Discuss students' answers. Explain that the graph shows that Coca-Cola's American market share is ⅔, or 66.6 percent.

Next, ask students to recall what they learned about competition in Chapter 5. How would they describe Coca-Cola's place in the American soft-drink market? (monopolistic competition) How do they think Coca-Cola got to that position? (advertising)

Then have students work in pairs to read the definitions of export and import (page 171) and reread the definition of specialization (page 168). Ask students to answer questions 8-10.

Absolute and Comparative Advantage (pp. 171-173) On a world map, show students where Jamaica is located. Tell them that Jamaica has one of the world's largest natural supplies of bauxite, which is used to make aluminum. Because Jamaica has so much more of this metal than most other countries, it is said to have an absolute advantage.

Then show students where the Netherlands and Kenya are located on the map. Tell students that both countries grow flowers, but because Kenya can grow flowers more easily and at less cost than the Netherlands, it is said to have a comparative advantage.

Multicultural Note

Africa is rich in natural resources. Nigeria exports petroleum. Zaire and Zambia have large copper deposits. Because of the lack of water in sub-Saharan Africa, many plants do not thrive and food must be imported.

In small groups, have students read the "Absolute Advantage and Comparative Advantage" section. Ask them to describe in their own words the difference between these two advantages. Have the groups answer questions 11-14. Then ask each group to make up fictitious countries and products to illustrate each term. Have a spokesperson from each group report the group's examples.

Next, explain to students the relationship between international trade and foreign currency and exchange rates. Explain that U.S. products are sold in other countries in foreign currencies, not U.S. dollars, and vice versa. Ask students to tell what they know about foreign currencies. Then ask students to call out the name of a country and its currency. List students' suggestions on the chalkboard. Following is a table listing some countries and their currencies that you might tell students to get them started.

Country	Currency
Brazil	cruzeiro
Cambodia	riel
Germany	mark
France	franc
Ghana	cedi
Mexico	peso
North Korea	won
Vietnam	dong

Some students may have had experience traveling to other countries and exchanging currency. Ask these students to tell about their experiences and to share examples of the currency with the class.

Have students read the "Foreign Currency and Exchange Rates" section. Point out that rates of exchange were fixed until the early 1970s, but they are now flexible. Explain that exchange rates are determined by the laws of supply and demand that they learned about in Chapter 3 and that the rate of exchange can change from day to day.

Think About It! (p. 173) Draw students' attention to the chart. Point out that the first column gives the country and the name of its basic unit of money. The second column gives the factor to multiply by to change that country's currency to U.S. dollars. For example, if you give the bank $10 Canadian, the bank will give you 10 x 0.785 or $7.85 in U.S. currency. If you want to buy $10 in Canadian money, the bank will sell it to you for 10 x 0.815 or $8.15 in U.S. dollars. Work through a few more examples using the pound and yen to help students understand the exchange rates and give them an idea of the relationship between each of these currencies. Ask students to answer questions 15-16 independently.

Multinational Corporations (pp. 173-174) Have students work in pairs to read the "Multinational Corporations" section. Ask students to brainstorm corporations that do business in foreign countries. Students should name such multinational corporations as McDonald's, Pizza Hut, Pepsi-Cola, Kodak, 3M, General Motors, and General Foods. Then have students complete questions 17-19 either independently or in small groups.

Free Trade vs. Restricted Trade? (pp. 174-177) Divide the class into six groups. Assign two groups to each of the following "protection" groups: protection of domestic jobs; protection of "infant industries"; and protection of national security, tariffs, quotas, and embargoes. Have each group read its relevant portion of the "Free Trade or Restricted Trade?" or "How Do Governments Restrict Trade?" sections. After they've read the sections, give the groups 15 minutes to prepare an explanation and example of their term to present to the class.

Explain to students that free trade means open business competition among nations, not free goods. Tell them that there are three reasons why governments might not want free trade or might want to limit the number of foreign-made goods sold in their countries. Have the three "protection" groups make their presentations to the class.

Based on the presentations, have students complete questions 20-23 either independently or in their groups.

Agreements on International Trade (pp. 177-178) Divide the class into four groups. Have two groups study NAFTA, with one group developing arguments for it and the other arguments against it. Do the same for GATT. Give the groups 15 minutes to read their relevant portions of "Agreements on International Trade." Then have each group present its arguments in a panel-discussion format. You may wish to take an informal vote among students to see how many favor each side of these issues. Finally, have students answer questions 24-28 in their groups.

Using Economics Skills (p. 179)

Point out to students that picture graphs often appear in newspapers and magazines because they are visually interesting. Explain that the key to understanding a picture graph is to find its "key"—the explanation of what the graph and numbers represent.

Some students may have trouble reading numbers larger than one million. Remind students that 500 million is the same as 500,000,000. Show them that 7 x 500 million is the same as 3,500 million, which is 3,500,000,000. This number is read 3 billion 500 million.

Have students work in small groups to answer questions 1-5. Ask the groups to share their answers for question 4 because there will probably be a variety of responses.

Guided Discussion Topics

Use the following questions to focus students' attention on the chapter's main points.

- Think of movies that you have seen recently. Were any particular brands of food or clothing visible in the movies? U.S. movies are popular in many different countries. How do you think brand names in movies affect sales of those products?
- Coca-Cola makes agreements with bottling companies in other countries instead of shipping its own bottles or cans. What are the advantages of this system?
- What is the value of foreign markets to U.S. companies?
- Give an example of how Coca-Cola tailors its advertisements for different markets.
- Give an example of a positive and negative result of international trade.
- What does specialization mean with regard to international trade?
- How does a change in the rate of exchange between two countries affect trade between those countries?
- Why are some people opposed to free trade? Why are others in favor of it?

Chapter 10 Review (pp. 180–181)

Assign the Chapter Review to be worked on in class. Have students independently or in pairs complete questions 1-15. You may wish to discuss the answers as a class.

Chapter 10 Test Answers

(1 point for 1-10; 2 points for 11-12; 3 points for 13-14)

1. a **2.** a **3.** c **4.** c **5.** b **6.** Specialization **7.** comparative **8.** multinationals **9.** subsidiary **10.** exports **11.** Protection of domestic jobs, protection of infant industries, protection of national security **12.** An embargo is the complete restriction of certain imports or exports.

Chapter Review Project (p. 181) Have students begin work on the Chapter Review Project. As a class, brainstorm the names of multinational corporations. Some possibilities are IBM, SONY, General Motors, Shell, and AT&T. Then divide the class into groups to investigate one multinational. The groups should decide how to do the research and present the information.

Have groups make their presentations on the multinational corporation that they researched.

Next, have students look back at the lists of U.S.- and foreign-made products that they generated before reading the case study. Students should now be better able to understand why some U.S. products are exported and some foreign products are imported. Discuss and revamp the lists in light of what students have learned.

Cooperative Learning Activities

1. Have students work in small groups to create a Coca-Cola timeline. Have them put important dates in Coca-Cola's history along the bottom of the timeline and important dates in U.S./world history along the top of the timeline. Display each group's work in the classroom or around the school.

2. Have students host a Coca-Cola party for another class during which they present what they've learned about the history of Coca-Cola and its success.

3. Have students work together to produce a foreign currency exchange poster. They will need to choose five countries and look up the present exchange rates of each in a national or big city newspaper. The poster should tell the name of the foreign currency and how it compares to the U.S. dollar.

13. Answers may vary. The country must have human resources in the form of highly trained workers, capital resources to manufacture the different computer parts, and sophisticated technology. **14.** Advertising can create demand. People can be convinced that buying a certain soft drink will increase the amount of fun they have or how cool they look. They can also be convinced that the taste is very desirable.

CHAPTER 10 TEST

Circle the letter of the best answer.

1. A tax on imported goods imposed by the government is
   a. an excise tax.
   b. a tariff.
   c. a quota.
   d. an embargo.

2. A nation that can produce more of a product than another nation using the same amount of resources has
   a. an absolute advantage.
   b. a comparative advantage.
   c. a free trade.
   d. a restricted trade.

3. Limits on the value or number of certain imported goods are
   a. tariffs.
   b. restrictions.
   c. quotas.
   d. embargoes.

4. A trade agreement among Canada, the United States, and Mexico is
   a. GATT.
   b. OAS.
   c. NAFTA.
   d. NATO.

5. The value of money that is determined by supply and demand is
   a. a fixed rate of exchange.
   b. a flexible exchange rate.
   c. an international trade.
   d. capitalism.

Complete each sentence.

6. _____ results when a person or country focuses on producing one product or a few products.

7. A nation has a _____ advantage over another if it can produce a product at a lower opportunity cost than its trading partner.

8. Large corporations that conduct business in many countries are _____.

9. A company that is owned by a larger corporation is called a _____.

10. Goods sold to other countries are _____.

Answer the following.

11. Name three reasons why governments might want to restrict trade.

_____
_____
_____
_____

12. What does embargo mean?

_____
_____
_____
_____

13. Suppose a country specializes in making computer parts and exports a large number of them. What can you guess is true about the resources of that country?

_____
_____
_____
_____
_____
_____

14. Soft drinks are not necessities. How do you think Coca-Cola was able to become such a large profit-making company from the sale of soft drinks?

_____
_____
_____
_____
_____
_____
_____

ANSWER KEY

Chapter 1:
Understanding Economics

1. study of how people use limited resources to produce goods and services
2. products that people use
3. activities that people do for other people
4. vegetables, herbs, salad dressing
5. Possible answers: electricity, telephone, computer services, city water system

Possible answers:

6. clothes — bank
7. food — dentist
8. stamps — bus or train
9. Microeconomics is the study of economic decision-making by individuals and businesses while macroeconomics is the study of the economy as a whole.

Possible answers:

10. food — CD player
11. air — a trip to Jamaica
12. shelter — car
13. water — leather jacket
14. clothing — basketball sneakers
15. Needs are items people can't do without while wants are items people desire but don't need.
16. Possible answers: education, a car
17. herbs, vegetables, salad dressing
18. picking, bundling, and packing
19. selling vegetables, salad dressing
20. Resources are what people use to create goods and services.
21. renewable and nonrenewable
22. soil, air, water
23. Melinda, Tammy, students
24. hoes, telephones, computers
25. No, the resources are interdependent.
26. capital, human, and natural resources used to create goods and services
27. By creating a good/service/business that becomes popular.
28. Possible answers: They have a popular product; They make a profit; They were the first student-owned, student-run natural foods company in the United States; They had an idea and took a risk.
29. sum total of all methods used to create goods/services
30. manufactured and bottled salad dressing
31. Because they needed another product to expand their operation and didn't have the resources/experience to bottle dressing.
32. when people want more goods and services than they can have
33. vegetables, herbs, salad dressing
34. It grows some of the ingredients, then it has it made and bottled by Sweet Adelaide.
35. 30,000 cases
36. grocery/natural food stores, farmers' market
37. Possible answer: not going to my friend's house so I could baby-sit for my little sister

38. what is given up when you make an economic choice
39. to make the best economic decisions
40. Possible answers: hanging with friends, playing sports, working at a part-time job

Using Economics Skills

1. 450 cases
2. May
3. about 200 cases
4. about 4,100 cases

Review: Vocabulary

1. goods
2. services
3. wants
4. needs
5. factors of production
6. entrepreneurs
7. natural resources
8. trade-off

Main Idea

9. the study of how people use limited resources to produce goods/services
10. when people want more goods/services than they can have
11. What goods/services will be produced? How will the goods/services be produced? How much, or how many, will be produced? Who will get the goods/services produced?

Understanding Economics

12. Possible answer: What will be produced? T-shirts with school name; How will they be produced? white cotton shirts, colored dyes, silk-screen printing; How many will be produced? 100 or one silk-screen's worth; Who will get the goods produced? students, faculty, friends of the school.
13. Possible answer: CD, cheeseburger with fries and drink, a book. I'd choose the fast food because it only costs $4.95. Then I can still buy a CD or a book, but not both.

Project

The following questions may be helpful in evaluating the projects: Did the students come up with qualities/statements of purpose that went with their business choices? Did they effectively express their business ideas?

Chapter 2:
Economic Systems

1. The way a society uses its resources to produce/distribute goods/services.
2. In China, the government decides which goods will be produced and how they will be distributed. In the United States, individuals and businesses decide what will be produced and how it will be distributed.
3. A system based largely on custom.
4. stability
5. It doesn't adapt quickly to change or create rapid economic growth.
6. Possible answer: They till the soil using horses as they have for hundreds of years.
7. Possible answers: the Shakers and some Native Americans. Because they live the way they have for hundreds of years.

8. A system in which a central agency controls the factors of production, decides what will be produced and how it will be distributed.
9. citizens supposed to be taken care of by government; increased sense of security
10. few economic choices; needs not always met
11. A system in which individuals and businesses decide what will be produced and how it will be distributed.
12. Possible answers: freedom to make personal economic decisions; encourages wide variety of goods/services; encourages entrepreneurs
13. lack of security, government is not there to help if business fails
14. Possible answer: command-run by a central agency, market-run by individuals and businesses
15. dictatorships—communist, fascist, military
16. command economic system
17. The fact that Marianna couldn't make her own economic decisions.
18. market—she could make her own economic decisions
19. A system that has features of command, traditional, and market economic systems.

Think About It! (p. 29)

In a tradition-based economic system, decisions are based on tradition.
In a command economic system, decisions are made by a central agency.
In a market economic system, decisions are made by individuals and businesses.
In a mixed economic system, decisions are made using a combination of all the systems.

20. actions of buying and selling
21. pay producers for products
22. pay individuals for productive resources to make products
23. individuals
24. allows individuals to make economic decisions in their own best interest
25. amount asked or paid for good/service
26. people trade freely with one another—sellers sell at price they choose and buyers free to buy or refuse to buy at that price
27. money made after all costs are paid
28. search for the greatest profit
29. when income is less than costs
30. property owned by individuals/businesses
31. rivalry between producers/sellers of similar products
32. Possible answers: raise/lower taxes, increase/decrease government spending, increase/decrease available loan money
33. by speeding up or slowing down the economy depending on what's needed
34. decreases amount of available loan money
35. increases amount of available loan money
36. Possible answers: national parks, national defense, benefits to veterans

Check Your Understanding (p. 34)

Protects: competition and property
Provides: national parks, veterans benefits, and national defense
Helps: raise or lower taxes, raise or lower spending, and raise or lower loan money

Using Economics Skills

1. China
2. U.S.
3. government
4. individuals/ businesses
5. U.S.
6. China

Review: Vocabulary

1. command economic system
2. mixed economic system

3. voluntary exchange
4. producers
5. economic system
6. market
7. market economic system
8. tradition-based economic system
9. consumers
10. capitalism
11. economic freedom

Main Idea

12. Possible answers: The United States' has a market economic system or capitalism. Economic decisions are made by individuals/businesses.

Understanding Economics

13. Possible answers: There are many similar stores and, therefore, much competition. I shop where I get the best prices.
14. Possible answer: Chuck must decide on a business; funding; location; and distribution. He will make these decisions himself because he lives in a market economic system. His decisions will be in his own best interest because he enjoys economic freedom.

Project

The following questions may be helpful in evaluating the projects: Did students have useful interview questions? Were they able to compare and contrast the economic system they learned about with the U.S. economic system?

Chapter 3:
Supply and Demand

1. amount of goods/services people are willing/able to buy at different prices
2. When three conditions are met: (a) want or need (b) willingness to pay (c) ability to pay
3. $18
4. $8
5. The lower the price, the more the demand.
6. increases
7. decreases
8. As pizza prices increased, demand decreased. As pizza prices decreased, demand increased.
9. when a relatively small price change affects the amount people are willing to buy
10. when a change in price has relatively little affect on the amount people are willing to buy
11. Possible answer: inelastic—Girl Scout cookies go up .50 cents a box. People still buy them because they don't just want the cookies, they want to support the scouts; elastic—baby-sitting up .50 cents an hour. People hired another baby-sitter because there were lots of sitters who would sit for less.
12. Inelastic: People view bread and milk as needs not wants. They will buy the same amount of bread regardless of price.
13. Elastic: Tacos are wanted, not needed. Demand of non-necessities is more tied to price.
14. Possible answer: People like Bo Jackson and Bo Diddley. They think they are cool and, therefore, the shoes are cool. That ups demand.

15. Possible answer: people's tastes, wants, cost of substitute product. The ad made Domino's "cooler" (people's taste) and, therefore, more desirable (people's wants); if you are going to spend $10 on pizza, you might as well buy "cool" pizza (cost of substitute product).
16. Domino's lost $200 in weekly sales.
17. Domino's lost $400 in weekly sales.
18. Domino's decreased its prices.
19. Both competitors' pepperoni pizza sales increased after the price dropped to $8.
20. Possible answer: Coca-Cola—cola—Pepsi—Dr. Pepper
21. Possible answer: Gap—casual clothes—J. Crew—Eddie Bauer
22. Possible answer: AT&T—long-distance service—MCI—Sprint
23. how much producers are willing/able to sell at different prices
24. as the price of a good rises, producers are willing to make more; as the price falls producers are willing to make less
25. producers are making more profit
26. it increases
27. It shows that as the price increases, so does production.
28. a relatively small change in price results in a relatively large change in the amount producers are willing to supply
29. Price changes have relatively little affect on both.
30. to make higher profit
31. Fixed costs do not change; variable costs change as production increases or decreases.
32. Possible answers: tomato crop failure, rise in price of flour, cheese, labor
33. Possible answers: rise in price of leather, labor, advertising
34. it would increase
35. price at which amount demanded equals amount supplied
36. demand increases; suppliers can't keep up with demand; the result is shortage
37. Shortages increase prices.
38. Surpluses decrease prices.

Using Economics Skills

1. ½ million boxes
2. ¾–1 million boxes
3. $4.50/box
4. $3 and $4
5. $5, $6 and $7

Review: Vocabulary

1. fixed costs
2. surplus
3. competition
4. law of supply
5. shortage
6. elastic
7. inelastic
8. law of demand

Main Idea

9. The higher the price, the more producers are willing to supply. The higher the price, the less consumers are willing to buy (and vice versa).
10. competition lowers prices.
11. When amount demanded equals amount supplied, you have equilibrium price.

Understanding Economics

12. productive resources including materials, wages, machinery, rent, advertising
13. lower prices
14. supply more or raise price

Project

The following questions may be helpful in evaluating the projects: Were students able to identify ways advertising persuaded them? Did they learn more about the power of advertising by listening to their classmates?

Chapter 4:
Government and the Economy

1. Possible answers: Government employs the most workers (about 16 million); spends the most money
2. young people are protected by minimum-wage, maximum-hour, and minimum-age employment laws.
3. federal, state, and local
4. federal
5. providing public facilities and services; providing public well-being/general welfare; regulating economic activity; ensuring economic stability
6. Possible answers: education; some health care; national defense; police and fire protection; public transportation; highways and bridges; and some hospitals
7. national defense
8. general welfare is the well-being of all citizens. The government tries to guarantee a minimum level of economic well-being for all its citizens, especially those in need. It provides benefits such as Social Security for the disabled, aid to orphaned minors, Medicare and Medicaid, and workers' compensation.
9. federal, state, and Social Security taxes
10. Government collects taxes for programs such as Social Security, Medicare/Medicaid, and workers' compensation that help people who are disabled or needy.
11. by passing laws, monitoring the marketplace
12. Possible answers: Fair Labor Standards Act, Equal Pay Act, Occupational Health and Safety Act
13. Equal Pay Act
14. The Federal Trade Commission, Food and Drug Administration, U.S. Postal Service
15. Environmental Protection Agency (EPA)
16. providing public facilities and services; providing for general welfare/public well-being; regulating economic activity; and ensuring economic stability
17. by regulating economic activity—ensuring that businesses meet clean air and water standards
18. Equal Pay Act—because by law men and women doing the same work must be paid the same salary
19. She earns less money.
20. A tax that takes a higher percentage of earnings from those with higher incomes.
21. A tax that takes a higher percentage of earnings from those with lower incomes.
22. how much a business earns
23. Because the taxes are on the items bought, not directly on the taxpayer.

24. An indirect tax is one not directly imposed on the taxpayer—for example, gas tax is on the gasoline. A direct tax is directly imposed on the taxpayer—for example, income tax.
25. a federal tax on imported goods
26. individuals
27. corporate and Social Security taxes
28. Gross Domestic Product
29. Economists add up the values of all final goods and services produced during a year.
30. peaks
31. when curve goes up
32. when curve goes down
33. When people who are willing and able to work can't find jobs.
34. A weak economy often increases unemployment.
35. a sustained rise in the average level of prices in a whole economy
36. a sustained fall in the average level of prices in a whole economy

Think About It! (p. 70)

Possible answers: unemployment—weak economy, seasonal jobs, jobs taken by machines; inflation—demand for goods and services grows faster than supply, costs of production rise

Using Economics Skills

1. individual income
2. 11 percent
3. all others

Review: Vocabulary

1. taxes
2. regressive tax
3. corporate taxes
4. inflation
5. direct taxes
6. progressive taxes
7. deflation
8. Gross Domestic Product
9. Consumer Price Index

Main Idea

10. Possible answers: regulating economic activity—ensuring competition, supervising working conditions, protecting consumers and the environment; ensuring economic stability—monitoring unemployment and inflation to keep economy stable; employing 16 million workers
11. with tax money it collects

Understanding Economics

12. Possible answer: I would make at least minimum wage because of the federal minimum wage law. I would pay federal income and Social Security tax, and I might pay state and city taxes. On my way to work, I would benefit from public transportation, and highways and bridges built by the government.
13. Possible ideas: public transportation, public library, fire department, police department, public schools

Project

The following questions may be helpful in evaluating the projects. Did the students work together to research the full range of services in the community? Did their report thoroughly investigate a service and include interviews with people who use it?

Chapter 5:
Business and the Economy

1. Possible answers: demand for your product, a shop, equipment, materials
2. Possible answers: advertising, records, employees
3. financial costs of running a business
4. money to start a business, or for other investment purposes
5. money paid for the use of someone else's money
6. a business owned by one person
7. a business owned by two or more people
8. a business owned by its stockholders
9. a state license allowing a corporation
10. People involved do not risk their own money and possessions like sole proprietors.
11. sole proprietorship
12. partnerships
13. Possible answer: A partnership. I would not be solely responsible, but I would have a lot of say in how the company ran. I'd share both profits and losses with my partners.
14. board of directors
15. carries out decisions made by the board of directors; heads all corporate divisions
16. from department heads via vice presidents
17. by issuing stocks and bonds to investors
18. dividends, selling stock for more money than they paid for it
19. no one buyer or seller has control over the price of a good
20. Because there are so many conditions to be met: all sellers offer same product, all sellers and buyers are free to enter or leave the market, there are many buyers and sellers of the product, there are no government restrictions, no one buyer or seller can control the price.
21. Bixby's Bikes
22. Classic Bicycles because they offer the best selling price.
23. Charlene's Cycles will sell more than Classic Bicycles because its price is much lower.
24. Possible answer: The market price will go down because of competition. The final price will be nearer that of Charlene's Cycles (maybe $200), but it won't be as low as Charlene's because that company is probably not making enough profit to stay in business.
25. when a single seller sells a product
26. seller must consider demand for a product
27. geographical, natural, technological
28. When you own a patent, you can set prices at whatever level the market will bear.
29. market dominated by a few competitors
30. Producers may set prices independently or follow prices set by industry leaders. In some cases, competitors may try to illegally fix prices.
31. Monopoly power gained on the strength of name and reputation. Loyal customers think there is no substitute for the product even though there are same/similar products on the market. Other examples: Kleenex tissue, Coca-Cola, McDonald's French fries.
32. corporations
33. partnerships
34. Profits are almost three times higher than sales (6 percent vs. 23 percent).
35. Sales and profits are same (75 percent).

Using Economics Skills

1. 8 percent
2. 1987

3. 3 percent in 1992
4. down
5. Because it had been losing money/market share for nine years.

Review: Vocabulary

1. financial capital
2. perfect competition
3. charter
4. sole proprietor
5. CEO
6. interest
7. partnership
8. monopoly

Main Idea

9. sole proprietorship, partnership, corporation
10. In perfect competition, no one buyer or seller has control over the price of a good.
11. Possible answer: Because they lead to higher prices and, possibly, inferior products. One seller has too much control over quality and price.

Understanding Economics

12. Possible answers: I would sell some of the company's stock rather than issue bonds because that way I would not have to pay the interest on the bonds; I would sell bonds and pay the interest rather than loose control of part of my 50 percent stock.
13. Consumer groups would be for the tighter laws because they would keep prices and products competitive.
14. Possible answers: lower the price per share; advertise

Project

The following questions may be helpful in evaluating the projects: Were students able to work together to create a charter application? Were students able to plan their election effectively? Were students able to pull the information together to create an organizational chart?

Chapter 6:
Labor and Pay

1. total number of people over the age of 16 employed or actively seeking work
2. In the 1800s most jobs were on farms, today most jobs are in cities.
3. White-collar, she performs "mental work" and the service she provides carries a fair amount of responsibility.
4. Blue-collar, they perform "physical work" and produce a good. Their jobs do not require advanced education.
5. master carpenters
6. white-collar
7. blue-collar
8. farm, fish workers
9. 57 percent
10. Professionals, they are highly educated and difficult to replace.
11. unskilled workers
12. skilled workers, professionals
13. low
14. somewhat—not as easy as unskilled, but easier than skilled
15. low-medium

16. special training and education
17. medium-high
18. no
19. very high
20. Because not all professionals are highly paid or difficult to replace, and not all semi-skilled workers are paid low wages and easy to replace.
21. The buyer is the business that hires the labor, the seller is the person offering his or her labor.
22. The higher the price of labor, the less that labor will be in demand or hired.
23. Buyers of labor also want to pay as little as they can. They want the most labor for the lowest wage.
24. the higher the wage, the bigger the supply of labor.
25. the higher the skill level, the higher the pay level
26. The less desirable and/or more expensive the location is, the higher the pay (and vice versa).
27. She has special, not easily replaced, skills.
28. groups of workers banded together
29. Possible answers: poor, unfair, unsafe, unhealthy
30. Possible answers: Unions won better working conditions (fewer hours, less danger) and higher wages for workers.
31. Possible answer: Employers might not favor a minimum wage increase because it would increase their costs.
32. Because the more expensive labor is, the less demand there is for it.
33. taxes and expenses subtracted from gross pay
34. taxes on income paid to the federal and some state and city governments
35. FICA or Social Security tax and 401ks. Possible answer: One (Social Security) is mandated by the government, the other is voluntary.

Using Economics Skills

1. $400
2. federal income Tax
3. 401k
4. $30.72
5. $80.85

Review: Vocabulary

1. net pay
2. blue-collar workers
3. professionals
4. gross pay
5. discriminate
6. pension
7. labor force
8. labor union

Main Idea

9. white-collar workers, blue-collar workers
10. demand, skill, job type, job location
11. mandatory deductions (income, Social Security, Medicare and, perhaps, state and local taxes.)

Understanding Economics

12. The supply of labor will increase and demand for it will decrease.
13. The disadvantage to (1) is the increased cost of labor, the advantages are less loss of production and the retention of trained, skilled, and highly skilled workers.

The disadvantages to (2) are lost production time and the fact that the company will probably end up paying some pay increase, the advantages are that the pay raise will probably be less than originally asked for and the retention of trained, skilled, and highly skilled workers.

The disadvantages to (3) are loss of production time while training new workers and loss of skilled and highly skilled workers, the advantage is lower labor costs.

Possible answer: I would choose (2) because it has the best chance of saving money while keeping a skilled work force.

Project

The following questions may be helpful in evaluating the projects: Were students able to work together to create a diverse list of jobs? Did students gather the information efficiently? Were they able to evaluate whether the pay for various jobs was fair?

Chapter 7:
Money and Banking

1. An economic system based on the direct trading of one good or service for another.
2. medium of exchange, unit of value, store of value
3. Disadvantages to the barter system: inefficiency—you end up with goods you don't need; difficulty determining value; no store of value—goods may spoil before you can use or trade them.
4. Money stores the value of the goods you sold because it holds its value for an indefinite period of time.
5. durable, portable, divisible, stable
6. Money needs to be easily carried so that it can be used wherever one is purchasing a good or service.
7. So that change can be made. Not being able to make change would be inefficient.
8. Yes. If it wasn't stable, or controllable, than the money supply could constantly increase and its value would decrease.

Check Your Understanding (p. 117)

Coconuts: yes, yes, yes, no
Reindeer: yes, no, no, no
Drums: yes, yes, no, no
Shells: yes, yes, yes, no

9. commodity, fiat, representative
10. It is valuable in itself.
11. The government gives it value.
12. personal checks, traveler's checks

Take Another Look (p. 119)

Traveler's checks: representative money
Silver ingots: commodity money
U.S. pennies: fiat money
U.S. dollar bills: fiat money
Personal checks: representative money

13. goods almost, but not exactly, like money
14. Possible answers: passbook savings accounts, CDs
15. With passbooks, you can withdraw your money without penalty at any time. With CDs, you pay a penalty if you withdraw your money before a certain time.
16. banks, savings and loan associations
17. Providing checking accounts to depositors. Banks are the main holders of the money in checking accounts and checks are the most widely used form of money in the U.S. economy.

18. money paid for the use of someone else's money
19. total value of currency and checkable deposits in the U.S. economy
20. by loaning money, providing checking accounts
21. oversee and regulate the U.S. banking system, supply currency, clear checks, control U.S. money supply
22. Too large a money supply can cause inflation; too small a money supply can cause deflation.
23. Possible answers: raise/lower the percentage of deposits banks must keep on reserve; raise/lower interest rates on money it loans; sell or buy back government bonds
24. a. Electronic Funds Transfer Act
    b. 1968 Truth in Lending Act
    c. Equal Credit Opportunity Act

Using Economics Skills

1. withdrawal, $26.13
2. adds deposit to old balance
3. 0675 4. $2,268.52

Review: Vocabulary

1. buying power
2. exchange
3. barter
4. fiat money
5. divisible
6. The Fed
7. commodity money
8. money supply

Main Idea

9. portable, divisible, stable, durable
10. savings accounts, checking accounts, loans

Understanding Economics

11. cash, personal checks, traveler's checks/ credit card
12. Possible answer: CD—If there was enough time for the CD to mature, it would be the higher interest earner. If there was not enough time for a CD to mature, an interest-bearing savings account would be better.

Project

The following questions may be helpful in evaluating the projects: Were students able to make a useful list of what to look for when choosing a bank? Did their chart do a good job of comparing services? Did they work together to reach a consensus on which bank to choose?

Chapter 8:
Investments and Your Future

1. To make a profit on the invested money.
2. stocks, bonds, mutual funds
3. common, preferred
4. interest-bearing certificate issued by a corporation or government that can be cashed in by a specific date
5. interest earned

6. 20 years
7. low risk
8. lower return than higher-risk investments 9. speculation, dividends
10. profits from sale or trade of investment
11. Preferred stocks guarantee dividends but offer no voting right. Common stocks don't guarantee dividends but do offer voting rights.
12. loss from the sale of an investment
13. two or more shares of stock given for each share owned
14. stock exchanges (NY Stock exchange, NASDAQ, American Stock Exchange)
15. middle person between buyer, seller
16. Call his broker, Anna Chung, and tell her that he wants to buy more shares of Nortec.
17. advantage: often less risk; disadvantage: often lower return
18. advantage: chance for high return; disadvantage: often more risk
19. company that pools together monies of many and invests it in stocks, bonds, or both
20. lower risk, lower expenses, increased earnings through expert buying/selling
21. general mutual fund—securities from diverse sectors; sector mutual fund—securities from a particular business sector
22. low-risk, big-company, general mutual funds are all lower risk than their counterparts.
23. manager with good record, experience
24. athletic footwear, general apparel, retail/specialty
25. Nike
26. To check its debt, sales, and earnings to help him decide if it was a wise investment.
27. record of the average performance of a large group of selected industrial stocks
28. bull market
29. 88
30. no
31. -3 ¼, loss
32. gained, 2
33. The main difference is more money in stocks for the younger person, more in bonds for the older person because a younger person has more time before retirement to make up any losses accrued in higher-risk stock investments.

Using Economics Skills

1. $60
2. 1992-1993 and 1994-1995
3. 1991

Review: Vocabulary

1. speculation
2. stock exchanges
3. preferred stock
4. stock split
5. bear market
6. capital gains
7. mutual fund
8. bull market

Main Idea

9. You can invest in higher-risk opportunities and there is more time for your investments to grow, earn profits.
10. stocks, bonds
11. Bonds are lower-risk investments.

Understanding Economics

12. Possible answers: I would invest it in bonds because I wouldn't have time to make up any losses I might have with stocks.

I would want a higher return, faster so I would invest it in stocks rather than bonds.
13. Possible answer: I would invest in a company that I knew had a popular product (Nike, the Gap), was stable and well-run. I would choose a business that consistently made a good profit.

Project

The following questions may be helpful in evaluating the projects: Did students research their stocks thoroughly? Were they able to effectively explain why they made their stock choices?

Chapter 9:
Consumers and Economic Decision Making

1. Possible answers: clothes, food, music
2. clothing, medical, transportation, taxes
3. savings, other
4. Possible answers: Clothing—you could stop buying clothes for awhile. Transportation—you could sell your car and take the bus. Food—you could eat out less often.
5. When you need and item and can afford it.
6. When you ask: Do I need it? Can I afford it? and one answer is yes and the other is no.
7. Possible answer: Do I need new sneakers? (no); Do I really want new sneakers (yes); I decide I probably shouldn't buy new sneakers.
8. Do I need a slice of pizza? (yes, I am starving); Can I afford a slice of pizza? (yes); I decide to buy a slice.
9. Do I need to buy a birthday present? (yes) Can I afford a present? (yes, but only if it's less than $20); I decide to buy it.
10. $20
11. Possible answers: spend less on clothes, recreation, savings (for one month)
12. Possible answer: Friends—It's easy to ask friends and I trust their judgment.
13. Possible answers: Friends are the most reliable, they care; consumer publications are reliable because they are impartial.
14. comparing prices for the same product at different stores
15. Possible answer: I'd visit different computer stores to compare brands and prices.
16. features, price, and type
17. Possible answer: Because you research, gather information, and learn all you can before the big test—putting your money down.
18. Possible answers: Max might have spent more money than he wanted to.
19. To protect them against loss or harm from products
20. safety, information, choice, hearing, re-payment
21. Decide if you want your money back, an exchange, or a repair.
22. firm, calm
23. It has consumer features, investigates and exposes bad products and unfair business practices, helps consumers resolve complaints.
24. departments of consumer affairs
25. attracting customers with a low-priced item and then switching it with a higher-priced item
26. Consumer Product Safety Commission
27. ones involving smaller sums of money
28. Legal Aid
29. speak to store's manager
30. contact the manufacturer
31. shop around for best deal

Using Economics Skills

1. Superspin
2. B-line
3. Superspin
4. 10 ounces
5. Possible answer: Classic because the price is much lower than Superspin, but the features rank almost as high.

Review: Vocabulary

1. necessity
2. comparison shopping
3. bait and switch
4. Better Business Bureau
5. luxuries
6. budget
7. unfair business practices
8. consumer rights

Main Idea

9. Possible answers: friends, observation, consumer magazines, advertising, comparison shopping
10. Possible answers: safety, information, choice, hearing, repayment
11. Possible answer: Better Business Bureau, Consumer Product Safety Commission

Understanding Economics

12. Possible answer: No. The seller is not obligated to repair my mistake.
13. Possible answer: Yes. If the manufacturer claimed it was waterproof than the seller should back the claim and repair it.
14. Possible answer: First, I would decide if I wanted my money back, an exchange, or a repair. Then I would learn the store's policies, gather my receipts and warranties and go to the store and make a complaint. If I got no satisfaction from the manger of the store, I would contact the product manufacturer. If I still got no satisfaction, I would contact the Better Business Bureau.

Project

The following questions may be helpful in evaluating the projects: Were students able to work together to identify a product and rating method? Were the criteria students used to rank products meaningful? Did they test at least four brands?

Chapter 10:
The Global Economy

1. trade between nations or between companies of different nations
2. Possible answers: new goods, noted discoveries, cultural advancements, historic tragedies
3. Countries have different resources.
4. Each country produces some products more efficiently than others, trade between the countries benefits all.
5. advances in communication, transportation
6. percentage of market held or controlled by one company or country
7. 2/3
8. When a country focuses on producing one or a few products rather than producing everything to satisfy its wants, needs.

9. Goods sold to other countries.
10. Goods bought from other countries.
11. When a nation can produce more of a product than another nation using the same amount of resources.
12. When a nation can produce a product at a lower opportunity cost than its trading partner.
13. Because Zimbabwe can grow flowers more efficiently, at a lower cost than the Netherlands.
14. The money made from exporting flowers is used to import food. Consumers in Zimbabwe are better off because they will now pay less for the imported food.
15. A fixed rate is set against one standard, a flexible rate means the value is decided by supply and demand.
16. The bank buys it for one price and sells it for a higher price.
17. large corporation that do business in many countries
18. Possible answer: Nike moves into India and goes into partnership with an Indian shoe manufacturer. Nike contributes its product line, the Indian company contributes its manufacturing plant.
19. Possible answer: Coca-Cola will contribute its product and advertising, Refresk will contribute its bottling plant and knowledge of its market.
20. To protect: domestic jobs, infant industries, national security
21. tariffs, quotas, and embargoes
22. They both limit imports.
23. Embargoes can be imposed on both imports and exports (quotas are just on imports) and are aimed at specific countries, not goods (quotas are aimed at goods).
24. Possible answers: To make trade between the United States, Canada, and Mexico as barrier-free as trade between California and New York. To stimulate the countries' economies by increasing the trade of goods and resources among them.
25. They think it will stimulate U.S. economy.
26. They think it will take away U.S. jobs and perpetuate poor safety and environmental conditions in Mexico.
27. General Agreement on Tariffs and Trade—it provides for much freer trade among many of the world's nations.
28. It involves many more nations.

Using Economics Skills

1. 2 billion
2. 375 million
3. European community and Pacific region
4. Africa, North Eastern Europe, Middle East, Canada—because there is room for Coca-Cola sales growth in these countries
5. 23.25 x 500 million or 11.6 billion

Review: Vocabulary

1. imports
2. quotas
3. absolute advantage
4. embargoes
5. exports
6. free trade
7. GATT
8. fixed rate of exchange
9. NAFTA
10. comparative advantage

Main Idea

11. Countries import what they don't specialize in and export their specialties making more goods available to everyone.

12. quotas, embargoes, and tariffs
13. Possible answers: To protect jobs, infant industries, national security, the environment

Understanding Economics

14. Possible answer: Volvo cars; in Sweden; yes—Ford, General Motors, Chrysler; higher safety record
15. Possible answer: Levi jeans; successful in the United States, unrivaled in most other countries, popular with foreign visitors; markets just beginning to open up to the United States like China and some Eastern European countries.

Project

The following questions may be helpful in evaluating the projects: Did students thoroughly research their multinationals? Did they organize and present their data effectively? Did they use visual aids?

LESSON 1

Name _____

Date _____

Work in small groups.

Suppose that every weekend a farmers' market sets up shop in your community. Your school gets permission to run a bake sale every week at the market. The money earned will be shared by all the after-school clubs.

As a group:

1. Decide on several items to bake. List them here and explain why you chose them.

2. Get recipes and make a shopping list. Write the shopping list and determine costs.

3. Determine the source of your first week's supplies. Will you borrow money to buy ingredients? Ask for donations? Explain.

4. Make a work schedule for four consecutive weeks. Who will work on what tasks and when?

5. Estimate the profit that you will make in four weeks. Show how you got your estimate. Show costs, number of units, and selling price per unit.

© Globe Fearon Educational Publisher

LESSON 2

Name _____

Date _____

Research project

Choose two countries other than the United States and complete the following:

Country 1

Name: _____ Continent: _____

Type of economic system: _____
_____

Major agricultural products: _____
_____
_____

Major manufactured products: _____
_____
_____

Leading trade partners: _____
_____
_____

Per capita income: _____
_____

Country 2:

Name: _____ Continent: _____

Type of economic system: _____
_____

Major agricultural products: _____
_____
_____

Major manufactured products: _____
_____
_____

Leading trade partners: _____
_____

Per capita income: _____

Sources of information you used:
_____
_____

© Globe Fearon Educational Publisher

LESSON 3

Name _____

Date _____

Television ads are often directed at particular groups. Companies advertise during television programs that appeal to people who are potential consumers of their products. To see how this works, complete this advertising log for several types of television shows.

Sports event

Program watched: _____

Products advertised: _____

_____

_____

Situation Comedy

Program watched: _____

Products advertised: _____

_____

_____

Prime-time Drama

Program watched: _____

Products advertised: _____

_____

_____

Cartoon

Program watched: _____

Products advertised: _____

_____

_____

Now, describe one ad in particular. Tell what group you think the ad was directed at. What was the product? During which type of program did the ad appear?

_____

_____

_____

_____

© Globe Fearon Educational Publisher

LESSON 4

Name _____

Date _____

Research project

1. Find the answers to the following for your state.

    What is the minimum wage? _____

    What are the work restrictions on teenagers?

    _____
    _____
    _____
    _____
    _____

    What agency in the state or local government handles complaints about worker safety?

    _____
    _____

2. Answer the same questions for a neighboring state.

    What is the minimum wage? _____

    What are the work restrictions on teenagers?

    _____
    _____
    _____
    _____
    _____

    What agency in the state or local government handles complaints about worker safety?

    _____
    _____

    List your sources:

    _____
    _____

Note: A good source of information might be a personnel officer in a local company or the labor board of that state.

© Globe Fearon Educational Publisher

LESSON 5

Name _____

Date _____

Interview a small business owner. Record the following information.

1. How did you get the idea for this business?
   _____
   _____
   _____
   _____

2. What goods and services does your business provide?
   _____
   _____
   _____

3. What did you need to start your business? How did you get it?
   _____
   _____
   _____
   _____

4. What are your expenses? Which were one-time expenses? Which are ongoing expenses?
   _____
   _____
   _____

5. Has the business changed over the years? In what ways?
   _____
   _____
   _____

6. Who are your competitors? How do you handle competition?
   _____
   _____
   _____

7. How important is advertising in your business?
   _____
   _____
   _____

© Globe Fearon Educational Publisher

LESSON 6

Name _____

Date _____

Research project

Choose three jobs that interest you. On a separate sheet of paper answer the five questions for each job you chose.

Job #1: _____
1. Skills/education required?
2. Where can you find this job?
3. What is the starting pay?
4. What are the chances for promotion?
5. Are jobs in this field increasing or decreasing?

Job #2: _____
1. Skills/education required?
2. Where can you find this job?
3. What is the starting pay?
4. What are the chances for promotion?
5. Are jobs in this field increasing or decreasing?

Job #3: _____
1. Skills/education required?
2. Where can you find this job?
3. What is the starting pay?
4. What are the chances for promotion?
5. Are jobs in this field increasing or decreasing?

Note: Use the Occupational Outlook Handbook, published by the U.S. Department of Labor.

© Globe Fearon Educational Publisher

LESSON 7

Name _____

Date _____

Use a calculator. Fill in the missing transactions in this checkbook record.

DATE	TRANSACTION	TRANSACTION AMT	NEW BALANCE
			$442.18
4/3/96	Gas Company	$42.56-	_____
4/3/96	Telephone Co.	$78.25-	321.37
4/3/96	Heating Oil	$140.00-	181.37
4/9/96	Paycheck	$356.21	537.58
4/9/96	Cash	$50.00-	487.58
4/9/96	Gift	$10.00	497.58
4/15/96	Rent	$475.00-	22.58
4/16/96	Paycheck	$356.21	378.79
4/16/96	Cash	$50.00-	328.79
4/20/96	Credit card	$60.00-	268.79
4/20/96	Car payment	$125.00-	143.79
4/23/96	Paycheck	$356.21	500.00
4/23/96	Cash	$50.00-	_____
4/25/96	Store charge	$75.00-	_____

1. How much does this person have in the checking account at the end of the month?

   _____

2. This person makes a $60 minimum payment on his credit card each month. Would you advise him to pay more or less? Suggest how much he could afford to pay per month to the credit company.

   _____
   _____
   _____
   _____
   _____

© Globe Fearon Educational Publisher

LESSON 8

Name _____

Date _____

Interview someone you know who works for a large company. On a separate sheet of paper, answer the questions that follow for each person you interview.

Name: _____

Do you have a retirement plan through your job?

How does the plan work?

Did you have a choice of plans?

How did you decide which plan to choose?

What other retirement plans have you made outside of work?

Interview someone you know who works for a small business or is self-employed.

Name: _____

Do you have a retirement plan through your job?

How does the plan work?

Did you have a choice of plans?

How did you decide which plan to choose?

What other retirement plans have you made outside work?

Interview an adult you know who is retired.

Name: _____

How did you plan for your retirement?

Are you happy with how it has worked out?

What advice would you give a young person planning for retirement?

© Globe Fearon Educational Publisher

LESSON 9

Name _____

Date _____

Choose an item that you would like to purchase.

Item: _____

1. **a.** List people and places from which you can get product information.
   _____
   _____
   _____
   _____

   b. Based on this information, which brand and style would you choose?
   _____

2. Comparison shop. Find your item in at least four different stores. Fill in the table.

Store	Item Available?	Price?	Warranty?

3. **a.** What is your final decision about what to buy and where?

   b. Do you think the time that you spent comparison shopping was worthwhile? Explain.
   _____
   _____
   _____
   _____

© Globe Fearon Educational Publisher

LESSON 10

Name _____

Date _____

Research project

Choose one country on each of the following four continents. Research the import/export and currency information for each.

Africa   Country: _____

Goods imported

Goods exported

Currency

Rate of exchange with U.S. dollar

Asia   Country: _____

Goods imported

Goods exported

Currency

Rate of exchange with U.S. dollar

Europe   Country: _____

Goods imported

Goods exported

Currency

Rate of exchange with U.S. dollar

South America   Country: _____

Goods imported

Goods exported

Currency

Rate of exchange with U.S. dollar

© Globe Fearon Educational Publisher